DEVOTED TO THE TRUTH

DEVOTED
TO THE
TRUTH

DEVOTED
TO THE
TRUTH

M. FETHULLAH GÜLEN

Foreword by

SIMON ROBINSON
&
MOHAMED ABDALLAH EL-SHARQAWY

Published by Tughra Books
335 Clifton Ave.
Clifton, NJ, 07011, USA
www.tughrabooks.com

ISBN: 978-1-59784-954-8
Ebook: 978-1-59784-989-0

Library of Congress Cataloging-in-Publication Data

Names: Gulen, Fethullah, author.
Title: Devoted to the truth / Fethullah Gulen.
Description: Clifton : Tughra Books, 2023. | Includes index.
Identifiers: LCCN 2022051716 (print) | LCCN 2022051717 (ebook) | ISBN
    9781597849548 (hardcover) | ISBN 9781597849890 (ebook)
Subjects: LCSH: Islamic ethics. | Gülen Hizmet Movement.
Classification: LCC BJ1291 .G848 2023 (print) | LCC BJ1291 (ebook) | DDC
    297.5--dc23/eng/20230301
LC record available at https://lccn.loc.gov/2022051716
LC ebook record available at https://lccn.loc.gov/2022051717
Printed in India

CONTENTS

CONTENTS

FOREWORD

It is a great privilege to write a foreword for this collection of essays by Fethullah Gülen. Over the last decade and more life has been hard for Gülen and for the Hizmet movement, and these essays provide an insight into how he and they have been able to keep going in the face of so much pain.

First, despite the ongoing conflicts there is no hint of self-righteousness or self-justification. There is no attempt to "join battle" with opposing forces. On the contrary, he keeps going back to the core message he has been preaching for a long time: depend upon God, for all good things come from Him; look to yourself and how you see the world, because the bad things come from inflating the self; look to the created world and reach out in compassion and peace, because there, in the practice of love, we will find God. This is the engine room from which the Hizmet has sought to stay focused and evolve as a global movement, focused on peacebuilding, dialogue, and critical reflection.

Second, these essays also remind us that whilst Gülen is a great scholar he does not spend time on asserting systematic theology. It is a great temptation for theologians of all faiths to justify their particular view of faith; to win the theological argument. Gülen, however, remains, at heart, a preacher, who is focused on spirituality and practice. His focus is on self-reflection (see five chapters on the "self"), the fostering of the virtues (see especially his chapter on "pity") and putting those virtues into action; working at taking responsibility for the self and for others.

His chapter on "pity" is important. He spends time urging us to have pity on the oppressors. It would be easy to see this as asserting the moral high ground against his oppressors. But two things work against that. His view of "pity" is not a condescending or assertive one, but one of genuine empathy and compassion. Then, most tellingly, he urges us to have pity with ourselves. We, too, can be seen as oppressors. We, too, need empathy and compassion, both of which are offered by God, and both of which we need to offer to ourselves and each other. Hence peace-building lies at the heart of Gülen's vision.

The real battle then is not so much between ourselves and those who oppress us, but within ourselves, as we seek to remain open to God, avoiding any inflation and over-assertion of the self, and open to each other, even those styled as enemies.

Gülen's focus on spirituality in action means that no one can claim to have the whole truth, and that truth is found in ongoing dialogue with others, other faiths, and secular institutions. "Devotion to the truth" then demands the capacity to listen, to hear that truth, in scripture and in science, in the environment and in each other. Such dialogue provides the basis of hope for the Hizmet Movement, as it explores its global identity, and for wider society, as it faces up to its ever-present challenges and conflicts in the years to come.

—**Rev. Prof. Simon Robinson** / Emeritus Prof. of Applied and Professional Ethics, Lecturer at Leeds Minster, Honorary Fellow at Uni. of Leeds
Epiphany 2023

***

In the name of God, the Most Gracious, the Most Merciful
When I first heard of Mr. Fethullah Gülen's name, I did not dwell on it much—there are thousands of authors, scholars, and preachers in Egypt! I remained mostly ignorant of Mr. Gülen until I discovered a book entitled "A Dialogue of Civilizations" by an American professor, Dr. Jill Carroll. The title caught my attention, and when I read it, I discovered a person of inspiration with fascinating insights into the fields of knowledge, education, and *islah* (restoration). Dr. Carroll stud-

ied Gülen's thoughts by putting him in "dialogue" with prominent philosophers: Gülen and the German philosopher Kant on "inherent human value and moral dignity"; Gülen and John Stuart Mill on "Freedom"; Gülen, Confucius, and Plato on "the ideal human being" and the value of "education"; and Gülen and Jean-Paul Sartre on "responsibility."

After finishing the book, I was very surprised and asked myself: how is it possible that a contemporary Muslim thinker is being discussed by Western academia and placed in the context of great philosophers, while someone like me (head of a university department) isn't aware of him? I feared that Dr. Jill Carroll might have been enamored with the man and went too far in praising him.

I thought I must get to know the man's ideas for myself, read his books translated into Arabic and English, and then learn about his biography, his activities, and his civil restorative movement. I initially read three of his books. The first was a biography of Prophet Muhammad (peace be upon him) published in Arabic as "The Eternal Light: Pride of Humanity"; a book which I'd call one of a kind in the literature of *seerah*, the discipline of the biography of the Prophet. The introduction was written by a great thinker, Professor Dr. Muhammad Imara, who described the book as "a unique work" written by "the distinguished scholar Muhammed Fethullah Gülen" "with the heart of a lover and the mind of a researcher, so it came in this glorious and beautiful manner that leads hearts and minds to the love of the master of all creation and following the example of the one with the great character."

I have read a great deal of the classical and contemporary books on the prophetic biography, but in "The Eternal Light," (*Al-Nur al-Khaled*) I found what I did not find in many other books. Gülen wrote it with both his mind and heart, in the true sense of the word, creating an inspiring, enlightening book that presents the social, political, military, psychological, and economic incidents of the prophetic biography in a new, rational, convincing, realistic, and practically reformist style—yet still deeply spiritual with grace. It is indeed, as our great thinker Muhammad Imara – may Allah have mercy on him – described it: a unique book in the noble prophetic biography.

Then I read his work on "Jihad in Islam" and was impressed by his broad horizons of understanding, explanation, analysis, and reasoning, as well as his deep deductive insights. I was eager to collect and read all of his books and writings that I could find. I had previously read the thoughts of Bediüzzaman Said Nursi, and I found that Fethullah Gülen had benefited greatly from his thoughts, some of which he developed, completed, carried forward into applicable programs. I also see him as an heir to the influential spirituality of Jalaluddin Rumi.

I was drawn to his writings, examining and contemplating them as a researcher specializing in philosophy and Islamic thought. I saw him as a free and independent thinker with a remarkable critical sense, along with objectivity, moderation, and a deep understanding of reality, its intricacies and complexities. I saw him as a diligent renewer in applying religious texts to changing realities and emerging situations. After reading Fethullah Gülen's thoughts, the bafflement that filled me when I read Jill Carroll's book, which I mentioned earlier, vanished.

Gülen's followers were inspired by his *islah*-oriented, civilizational, and innovative ideas, and they established a civil, educational, and social movement called the "Hizmet Movement." The name Hizmet—which means, literally, "service" in Turkish—was appropriate, due to the movement's aims at serving humanity in the fields of education and upbringing. People in Turkey and around the world welcomed this movement, and its schools, educational centers, and universities spread widely and significantly within Turkish society and beyond.

Gülen firmly believed that the Islamic community as a whole suffered from three chronic problems: ignorance, poverty, and division. He devoted himself to advocating for knowledge and working to activate a comprehensive educational project to address these major challenges effectively and decisively. He urged the wealthy to practice social solidarity, help the poor, invest in education, and adopt constructive dialogue as a means of resolving deep conflicts. He promoted a culture of coexistence, acceptance of differences and diversity, and spreading peace while reducing enmity and hostility through dialogue and understanding at the local, regional, and international levels. All of this was accompanied by an explicit condemnation and rejection of violence, fanaticism, and terrorism.

The Hizmet Movement's educational and humanitarian activities expanded locally, regionally, and globally, achieving noticeable successes at providing effective solutions to some of the problems currently facing humanity. The movement succeeded greatly in its noble endeavors and was able to present an attractive, civil, social, and cultural project based on the principles of Islam and its essential values and its lofty, tolerant spirit. In doing so, the movement followed the approach of Fethullah Gülen, aiming to achieve rational and mature Islamic authenticity in essence, spirit, and content, alongside contemporaneity in form, tools, and methods of work and activity.

I should mention that I traveled from Cairo to Istanbul to learn more about the institutions established by Hizmet, both in Turkey and internationally. I was delighted with what I saw: a model of great civilizational Islam and a civil society organization. I made sure to visit the residence where Gülen used to live. I found it to be a small room in a building dedicated to education, where he delivered lessons and sermons to his students. The room of the reformist thinker was very modest, with no bed, as he used to sleep on a mattress on the floor of that humble room, while the Hizmet schools, universities, and institutions were built to the best possible standards in Turkey and across five continents.

In this book, you will find everything I have talked about, including moderate and balanced thought and righteous deeds. May Allah place this in the balance of his good deeds and those who love him around the world.

And Allah is the purpose behind all.

—**Prof. Dr. Mohamed Abdallah El-Sharqawy** / Prof. of Islamic Philosophy and Comparative Religion, Faculty of Dar Al-Uloom, Cairo Uni. February 18, 2023 – Cairo, Egypt

PREFACE

L eaders emerge and make a difference in times of crisis. When hopes seem to be fading away on the horizon, leaders come forward to show people where to turn to; they remind them of their goals and navigate them to the right direction. They strive to ensure stability, set priorities, and maintain communication with those following him or her.

Fethullah Gülen's life has rarely been a life without crisis, a condition which perfectly aligns with Turkey, his home country. Turkish democratic experience shook to its foundations multiple times by military interventions from the 1960s until today. Each time, the regime suppressed the society by eliminating prominent figures who, they assumed, had a potential to challenge the status quo, regardless of whichever ideological, political, or religious camp they may belong to. In the early '60s when Gülen rose to the public scene as a young cleric with his heart-rending sermons and growing public outreach, he became a natural target of the so-called "guardians" of the Turkish regime. For them, he was going far beyond regular clerical duties, which were clearly identified as with any other "civil servant": lead the daily prayers and funeral services. Any community service after "working" hours, be it having Qur'an classes, conducting exegetical studies, a public lecture, or joining a friendly reading circle were not in the "job description" of a state-licensed preacher.

In his sermons, however, Gülen spoke on religion together with science, addressed challenging issues on faith, delivered lectures in conference halls and cafés and brought convincing explanations to the most confusing questions of the time. Those who listened to him felt empowered by this engaging and learned man of religion. To the regime, these activities were assumed to be crossing over the line and they made sure he suffered

13

the consequences: he was under constant surveillance throughout the '60s and '70s; got arrested after the military intervention of 1971; chased by the junta during the '80s. He was a major, if not the top, target of the so-called "postmodern coups" in the '90s and the 2000s.

Despite all of this persecution that spanned decades, Gülen was able to steer his ship through the wavy waters of Turkey and inspired tens of thousands of people to go abroad and open schools in hundreds of countries. His promotion of dialogue and understanding among peoples of the world has flourished as a faith-inspired social movement called Hizmet, which has been embraced both in Turkey and in other countries where these schools operated.

It is rare to find in history persons with a similar scope of influence to be ever left alone. In December 2013, a huge corruption scandal engulfed Recep Tayyip Erdoğan, then the Turkish Prime Minister, his family, and cabinet members. Accusations were serious: embezzlement of billions of dollars, violation of the United Nations' sanctions on Iran, misappropriation of government contracts, money laundering, defrauding the international banking system, bribes... This came during Erdoğan's third term when he was at the height of his power with a monopoly over the parliament and controlling the majority of the media. In a very short time, he was able to turn the tables by carving out a new narrative in which the corruption probe was projected as a coup attempt to topple him down by the usual suspects: Fethullah Gülen and Hizmet Movement. He went as far as to overhaul the entire judiciary and the police force, and started a nationwide crackdown on schools, foundations, corporates, and media organizations affiliated with Hizmet. In the aftermath of the staged (rather fake) coup attempt on July 15, 2016, Erdoğan, now allied with the oppressive Kemalist establishment – his former foes – accused Gülen and the people inspired by him as the culprits and initiated the greatest purge in Turkish history: around two million people investigated, six hundred thousand taken into custody, around a hundred thousand arrested, a hundred and fifty thousand dismissed from their government positions, almost two hundred media organizations and up to three thousand schools and dorms shut down – all of them lawfully opened and running, but now banned from operation because of their affiliations with Hizmet.

Devoted to the Truth is a compilation of articles Fethullah Gülen wrote since 2016 while this unprecedented purge was under way in full force. Each article, on its own and in connection with the other ones in the volume, is a source of deep knowledge and readers can benefit from them especially in relation to themes like commitment to truth, self-reckoning, and living a virtuous life. Still, being aware of the circumstances Gülen and the Hizmet community were in while he was writing them can be useful to have a deeper idea about the dynamics that might have shaped this book. While many readers who are familiar with these dynamics may make connections to certain metaphors and nuances more easily, the overall content is centered around certain aspects of human character, its weaknesses, and the ways to overcome them, which are universally relatable by all.

With this backdrop in mind, what we find in these articles is a seasoned leader who is going through all the blood, sweat, and tears of keeping his ship afloat, the crew and passengers safe and calm. When the world seems to be in darkness, we find Gülen calling out to his community that this "Eclipse" is over, and inspires them how to be "Travelers to the Light." As he leads his followers on this journey, he teaches how they should hold themselves to account by "Facing the Self." While feeling "Pity" for the perpetrators of all the persecution they are going through, Gülen shows the path on how to "Heal" and take action "So Others May Live."

ANOTHER ECLIPSE IS OVER

Our society is being challenged by a spiral of problems – a challenge of a rare kind. On the one hand, we are troubled by overwhelming misfortunes and catastrophes. On the other, we are being tested with countless urges that lead to depravation, contempt for values, decadence, a purposeless life, addiction to pomp and vanity, avarice and self-indulgence, desiring this world to the point of worshiping it and with false assumption that it lasts forever. To be able to attain these ambitions, we are told, we need to adopt a perspective that unscrupulously legitimizes all sorts of means in a Machiavellian way. While our hearts and souls are paralyzed by these devastating afflictions, many other cases of baseness come in the form of outrageous indifference, embarrassing heedlessness, being silent like "a mute devil"[1] in the face of sheer injustice, and closing our ears to the uproars of despots and oppressors and to the cries of innocents and victims. This level of wickedness has been rarely witnessed in history.

Notwithstanding all these concentric deviations, there have been a few dozen devotees of love who have always taken on all the risks and moved forward on their path of resurrection, even at the expense of their own lives and regardless of the bumpy road ahead. These devotees have

---

1   Ibn Qayyim al-Jawziya, *Jawab al-Kafi*, p. 69, 113; Nawawi, *Sharh al-Sahih al-Muslim*, 2/20. It is reported that Prophet Muhammad, peace be upon him, said, "That who sees injustice and remains silent is a mute devil" (i.e., a silent partner in that injustice).

17

tied their lives to the wellbeing of others and have always breathed with this lofty ideal. They say as Fuzuli said,

How pleasant to my soul if the Beloved asked for it,

What worth is my soul anyway that I should not sacrifice it for my Beloved

These devotees have lived these sentiments joyfully; they rose with hope and moved with disregard for worldly ambitions. As they took refuge in the All-Patient One, they never slowed down while marching on the path of the Prophets, despite all the complicated and insecure directions, unyielding hurdles, and merciless deviations. Never deterred by these challenges, they preserved the purity of the sacred in their hearts and the glory of their ideals. Never satisfied with the distances they covered, they asked for more and traveled to the four corners of the world to voice and exemplify the truth and love of the Divine.

When they first set out, they already knew compliance with the heavenly orders and prohibitions would not be easy. They knew there would be pitfalls ahead. They knew it was not a smooth highway they had chosen, but they were reassured that with the elixir of patience their heavy burden would become light enough to carry. As painful and indigestible as patience was in the beginning, its results have been sweet as sherbet. Patience is the elixir helping these devotees survive the vortexes of sins and carnality. With patience, they can remedy the malice of their persecutors and render ineffective the conspiracies of tricksters. Through the goggles of patience, they see that everything has a due time. They have patiently accepted the fact that this is a long walk, and the road will not come to an end soon. Patience has taught them to seek refuge in the infinite power of the Almighty. With patience, they have steered clear of the maddening bigotry of some fanatics who have fixated themselves on revenge, grudge, obstinacy, and envy. With patience, they have moved forward, calling others to brighten their minds with the "sunlight of knowledge" and to nourish their hearts with the "moonlight of faith."

When faced with a pressing situation, they have hung on by always turning to, *"O you who believe (believers who are people of security and trust)! Seek help (against all kinds of hardships and tribulations) through persevering patience and the Prayer; surely God is with the persevering and patient"* (al-Baqarah 2:153). This verse has served as a freshwater spring and healed their spirit from all kinds of afflictions. What a heavenly source of life this spring has been! A new Divine favor has been born in their hearts with each sip, gracing them with eternal life. Each drop has become an ocean.

They have been fully aware that their lives are transient and their strength limited. They have disassociated themselves from their individual powers – to the extent of their good judgment – and sought refuge under the unlimited strength of the Almighty and His Willpower, by way of which their drops turn to oceans and their atoms to suns. Indeed, what doesn't exist comes into existence, and what has no value becomes priceless, in this way. The Almighty's favors are also dependent on the self-effacing ones who have turned to Him. How wonderfully the following lines by a friend of God express this fact:

> *You do not manifest Yourself while I am appearing on the screen;*
> *The condition for Your self-disclosure is my self-effacement.*

Gavsi

These devotees of love have strived hard even during the direst of times: when time – time that has been detached from the One – has been disloyal and feelings have turned to delirium; when brute force has run amuck and pursuing a life of prophetic virtue has become extremely difficult. Through it all, they have continued on the path even when the future has become obscured. They have worked to generate humble resources, and built their own fountains. They did their utmost to inspire our hopes as they expanded wide as an ocean and then evaporated to precipitate as drops of mercy. The driest deserts and thorn fields have become gardens of roses. When there was no beam of light across the horizon, and roads were concealed without signposts, they illuminated the path of those left in the dark. They have been praised everywhere as the cavaliers of light. But their efforts have never been for praise; what they have received is the expression of love and gratitude.

Ultimately, it has been Divine favor upon them that they have come to be recognized for what great conquerors were unable to achieve. Despite all these achievements, they chose to comply with the principle of logic, "negating a negation is an affirmation," thus, in awareness of their impotence and poverty in relation to the Divine Majesty, they have humbly renounced themselves. The Almighty is the One who gives, and they are the honorable ones to receive. This is how they have formulated the matter, and they have done their utmost not to be disrespectful to the Most Honorable One by assuming any false pride, arrogance, extreme self-reliance, or self-praise. They have maintained their faithfulness and sincerity in being His servants by seeing His help, support, and protection behind all the grace. In the face of misfortunes and obstacles they have never fallen into despair or disappointment. They have galloped in all directions where the sun rises and sets, seeking to realize their ideal of carrying the Divine message, and to deserve the merits of being *"the perfect pattern of creation"* (at-Tin 95:4). This challenge has been no different than racing great distances under the scorching desert sun. But their ideals have been like the cooling shade of a spring rain. These ideals have been their provisions on this hard trip, keeping them alive and motivated, and enabling them to soar to their destination. God would never leave these sincere travelers of truth abandoned on their way.

As was the case for all their predecessors, their path has been obstructed by some intolerant bigots, who have been miserably impaired by billowing feelings of envy. They have launched organized defamation campaigns and attempted to destroy whatever God enabled the cavaliers of light to achieve. This extreme malice would not even be perpetrated by the most outrageous deniers of truth. Devils have rejoiced, for this level of persecution is unacceptable in all circumstances. But it is endorsed when inflicted on these devotees. Yet, the commitment of these devotees to attaining the Divine pleasure has made such destructive efforts ineffective; those marching on His path have devised alternative gateways to His contentment and have marched on without losing speed.

Time shrinks as they march, and the Earth, humbled under their feet, breathes life. Each spring turns into a waterfall, hopes grow firmer, and drizzles become downpours. Many surprise triumphs happen when failure seems unavoidable; murmurs of life are heard in the spiral of darkness; and many unexpected rays of light beam off celebrations in broken hearts. "God is with the truthful," whispers their common sense, in a quiet search for wisdom, as the following lines flow from within:

If still determined, no more despair

You overcame what was impassable before

And became a source of hope for all

Now, it's your turn to speak, I say no more…

F. Gülen

TRAVELERS TO THE LIGHT

Travelers to the light are the ones who have always endeavored to surpass mere corporeality. Apparent in the way they have lived has been a determination to bid farewell to lowly feelings. Focusing on their heart at all times, they have hastened to enjoy the horizons of their soul. They have always turned away from their own shadows and marched toward the source of all lights.

During an inauspicious period, when the masses suffered separations one after another and succumbed to darkness, when societies were stranded and stunted, people lost hope and were diverted from the path, these travelers to the light essentially taught all exhausted travelers the qualities and conditions of being privileged as "the best of creation." They invited the weary to self-respect, rousing the eyes and ears of those who had stopped walking on the path, and promising resurrection to lifeless hearts.

Thanks to their character with deep qualities and capacity to represent their values, over time, the abyss between where we are stuck and where we should be has become nothing more than a smooth plain. The seemingly insurmountable peaks have turned into highways, vast oceans became crystal clear waterfalls. The travelers to the light led the stricken, hopeless souls towards the horizon of light beams.

The travelers to the light were created from dirt and clay, too; however, after spiritual transformations, they took wing in tandem with the creatures of light. They lent their wings to those in their environment so they could soar towards the peaks of "annihilation in God" (*fana fillah*) and subsistence with God (*baqa billah*). These are realms with no ele-

23

ment or quality. Leaving their corporeal edifice a step behind and finding their metaphysical profundities far better, they ascended toward the inexplicable realms where angels welcomed them with greetings of peace and cheers of support.

Almighty God, with His Divine will, majestic might and power, perfect favor, and profound compassion, reciprocated their step toward Him with miles of proximity, bestowing innumerable favors on them for their turning toward Him, even if they just turned an inch. He conferred on them boundless Divine favors in return for their loyalty. He replied to their love and affection – regardless of how limited they were – with His infinite and boundless kindness. He poured upon them favors that no eye has ever seen, no ear has ever heard, and no mind has ever imagined, so much so that the travelers to the light ebbed and flowed between amazement (*hayra*) and stupor (*hayman*). They couldn't think of leaving that atmosphere, even for a while. How could they, when they always had an eye far beyond the horizons? When their hearts beat with eagerness for infinity and their emotions burst forth with the joy of love. Of course, as they ascended to the "inexplicable" peaks in heavenly realms, they – having conferred all that pertains to the carnal self to the nervous system and emotions – were filled with a profound sense of humility, modesty, and awe, and each was inversely proportional with their spiritual status. Sometimes, they sobbed and said:

> *If the All-Merciful One weighs my sins as they are,*
>
> *I fear the scales on the Day of Judgment will break.*

Sometimes they thoroughly criticized themselves:

> *I glanced at the universe's book of deeds,*
>
> *I have not seen any account with as many sins as mine!*

As opposed to these blessed seekers of truth, who run from one peak to another while still dedicated to the truth, there are also ill-fated, ever-shackled slaves of lust, fame, pomp, show, and power, following Satan and his posse. Since they have turned away from servanthood to God, they have gone after countless idols. Besides losing the Hereafter, they have turned their world into hell in unbearable stress, angst, and paranoia. They have lived with the fear and worry of losing all they have acquired, and by fabricating whimsical foes, they have engaged in fighting them, overtly and covertly. They have spent their power and strength on tyranny, injustice, domination, oppression, aggression, and molestation. They have stooped to the position of being more evil than the most damned tyrants.

Within the constant cycle of historical recurrences, the slaves of pomp, power, reign, and fame have always displayed parallel attitudes to one another. They have all resorted to similar tricks, fooled the masses with similar conspiracies, and eventually fell into a pit of their own digging. How nicely Sheikh'ul-Islam Ibn Kemal[1] puts it:

> *Do not hand over a pickaxe to your carnal self*
>
> *Lest you dig a pit on anyone's path*
>
> *If you do dig a pit on someone's path*
>
> *you will be the one who will fall into it headfirst!*

With no exception, the arrogant, egotistical bullies of the past perished in similar finales. Surely, today's fanatical and delirious tyrants, who disregard fairness, common sense, rights and justice, will meet the same end in the very near future.

In contrast to them, the radiant faces who are directed towards the right course always see the truth, think accurately, and strive to deliver others toward the truth. They lend a saving hand to those tripped and dragged by Satan. By showing them the signs along the road, the radiant souls inspire the shaken ones, orienting them toward the light. It is their indispensable wish to save those on the wrong path from the oppression of falsehood. It is their mission to deliver them to the joyous clime of truth and justice, hence crowning their lives with the sentiment and ideal of letting others live. No matter how dark days may turn, what distress weeks may bring, or what months may start and end in oppression, the radiant souls smile towards the future, believing:

---

1   Sheik'ul Islam Ibn Kemal was a sixteenth-century judge at the time of the Ottoman Sultan Süleyman the Magnificent.

The night is always gravid with joy and sorrow,
See what emerges from the womb of the night before the daybreak!

Rahmi

They walk on toward that sacred destination that is the object of their wishes and say, "Every night has its dawn, every winter has its spring." They walk on by seeing each trouble and predicament as a font of purification, heedful that domination and tyranny are two inseparable trials placed on the path of Prophets. Aware of walking towards infinity and turning down worldly offers, they walk toward eternity and reach beyond the world where the splendors of infinitude are apparent. They do so already intoxicated by way of contemplating the beyond.

May God bless the diligent travelers of this path thousands of times! Shame on the futureless, miserable tyrants who want to turn them away from this path!

DEVOTED TO THE TRUTH 1

Devoting oneself to communicating the truth is a requisite that comes with the privilege of "the perfect pattern of creation" (*ahsan al-taqwim*), an unparalleled status for those who can live up to it. There are devotees who take every opportunity to speak of God and to endear Him to others. They work hard to open the doors of people's hearts to God and to His Beloved Messenger, Prophet Muhammad, peace be upon him, who is a trustworthy avenue to attaining the Divine – an avenue, but as worthy as the destination. These devotees may not be aware of it, but they are being, and will be, applauded by the denizens of the celestial abodes.

The travelers on this path endear their Beloved to those they reach through their most convincing tools: their natural way of being and the way they epitomize their values. They always inhale the truth and spread it wherever they go. Hence, they attain Divine love, stage by stage. They adopt the Prophetic message to make the servants of God love Him, hoping to be loved by God in return.[1] They travel to the farthest corners of the globe, "the Beloved" on their lips. "God's love" in return for their efforts as promised in this prophetic narration is such a Divine grace that it is like a vast ocean in return for a drop of water; indeed, a priceless gift.

Being under the tutelage of the Prophet and following his footsteps is one of the foremost ways and means that lead a person to endear the Almighty. All who know and acknowledge the Prophet and enter his spiritual atmosphere are saved from inattentiveness as far as they in-

---

1   At-Tabarani, *al-Mu'jamu'l Kabir*, 8/90, 91; Ibn Asakir, *Tarihu Dimashk*, 24/72.

ternalize and live according to the light-diffusing scriptures from God's attribute of speech (*kalam*). Hence, they start seeing everything with insight. While their eyes watch the signs in the temple of the universe, their ears effervesce with zeal when they hear the miraculous word of God illustrating the laws of creation as they unfold in the huge sanctuary of existence and events. They respire by the following lines of the poet:

There is You, O Lord; there is You, once and always,

You are always in my mind, in my heart and in my soul!

They deeply weave together contemplations starting from faith (*iman*), knowledge of the Divine (*marifa*), love of the Divine (*mahabba*), and love and yearning for a reunion with God. They call upon the One murmuring the melodies portrayed and voiced by the language of existence and events. See how exquisite a man of love and elation put this experience into words:

The universe as a whole is a grand book of God,

Try any of its letters; the meaning of each reveals nothing but Him.

Recaizade Mahmud Ekrem

Hearing this voice, reading and understanding its immensely expansive message, requires a seeing eye, a hearing ear, a rationalizing reason, an unrestrained discernment and understanding, and a vast curiosity and love of knowledge. It is very difficult, rather impossible, for imitators who are entangled by the glaze of imitation and unable to jump over the fences of forms and figures to sense and eventually internalize this. When all neurons in the brain lack such an expansive sense of faith, and hearts lack sincerity and profundity, the light of Divine knowledge does not exist in this spiritual anatomy either. Love does not exist in a heart and soul where there is no light and illumination of the Divine knowledge. The breezes of ardent desire for reunion with God do not blow there.

Individuals who dedicate themselves to communicating His message and endearing Him to others enter the atmosphere of being loved in this way. They crown their lives with manifestations of presence in the

Divine. They passionately utter His names day and night, without committing any blunder, just as they continuously run the marathon of good
deeds. They strive to attain "sincerity." They quiver as they remember
"being under the constant watch of the Almighty"; as they contemplate
resignation to God they hasten from one vista to another for more reflection. Without being delayed by steep hills, deep vales, vast oceans,
and many other trials and tribulations, they march toward God's favor
and reunion with the All-Truth, without expecting anything corporeal
or ethereal. Individuals attaining this horizon watch with deep sorrow
those who are entangled by worldly pomp and fame. As they wail and
moan inwardly, they avoid the traps the unfortunate ones have tripped
over and move forward to rip love and interest for the vanities of life
from their hearts!

"*We hit the road immersed in Your love; we seek no (personal) glory!*" (Sayyid Nigari) they say, always mentioning Him. They consider the
most enchanting expressions as a waste of words if they are not about
Him and shift to talk about the Beloved. They scan the horizons observed
in their dimensions of the soul and inner secrets of their heart.

They know their willpower is connected with all of these feelings,
thoughts, and privileges, but only as an *un*necessary condition; they are
fully aware to credit everything to a distinct Divine favor and the exclusive will of God – they never compromise their faith in the Uniqueness of
God, for the sake of which they could renounce everything. According to
them, the confines of human willpower are very narrow: determination
and perseverance are not adequate causes; corporeality and bestiality are
handicaps blocking the path leading to real humanity. In the face of all
these, claiming all privileges as their natural right, they would acknowledge, is a sort of obscured blasphemy. Hence, notwithstanding all types
of achievements and rewards, they murmur the considerations of:

A slave as I am, I am not worthy of this gift

Why am I being granted this favor?

M. Lütfi

Attributing everything to the breadth of Divine compassion, the ex-
pansiveness of His favor, and His surprise manifestations, they acknowl-

edge that "*Everything is from You, You are the All-Sufficient / O Lord, I turn toward You!*" and hurry towards the heavenly audience with the Sultan of the Sultans, the One Who responds with His infinite favor.

Indeed, travelers of this blessed caravan have set out on this path to the Divine by first sealing the openings of their inner realms against anything other than Him; along the way they breathe in life from being in the Divine presence. Constantly engaged with the considerations of Him, they have not wanted to hear alien songs in the realms of their hearts and emotions. They started speaking by first reasoning that all words should be in reference to Him, each discourse should be rhymed by His mention, and each speech should be concluded by citing Him. Moreover, by considering all expressions and conversations that do not mention Him as waste of words, they made their discussions and consultations more profound by their talk of the Beloved. Almost always, they made the following considerations the voice of their inner excitement:

> *I wish all the creation in the world would love my Beloved,*
> *I wish our talk would always be about the Beloved...*
>
> Taşlıcalı Yahya

Saying, "*Either speak about the Beloved or stay silent / If you will, open your arms wide for only that!*" (the first line is from Fuzuli, the sixteenth-century Turkish poet), they completely seal their doors against strangers.

In contrast to those souls devoted to God on the path of Prophets, there are others who are deprived of a lofty goal in their lives. These egotistic victims of avarice, power-addicted, human-turned-aides of the devil have never quit maligning the devotees on the path to Him. These dark souls have used various methods of oppression and domination to annihilate the devoted souls – yet, they have been the ones annihilated. They have waged war against the light, which the Divine has endowed to the devoted souls who endeavored to represent it. They have lied and defamed, trying their best to block the path of the travelers to the light. However, they themselves have been defamed by means of their own wickedness and meanness, for the travelers of love and munificence have been following the footsteps of the Prophets and they are under the protection of God. Nobody will be able to eradicate those who have been scattered by God on the plain of service and have grown like seeds or ears of grain. Nobody can put out the torch lit by God. Because behind that illuminating torch is the mercy of God, the will of the All-Glorified, and the decree of the Beneficent Bestower of Bounties. How nicely Ziya Paşa[2] puts it:

> *What God decreed cannot be reversed by force,*
>
> *A candle He kindled cannot be extinguished by blowing of course!*

It may be said that the wrongdoers have revived the practice of the hypocrite Ibn Salul,[3] yet in vain was their endeavor! Because behind the travelers of Truth is the help of God:

> *God, the beauty of Whose glory is apparent in all corners,*
>
> *In hearts is a shadow of that manifestation;*
>
> *Sensing this, we wander and seek Him everywhere,*
>
> *And the sweetest memories loom before our eyes.*
>
> *Each color, voice and pattern is an expression of His existence...*

May God speed you, O the valiant souls devoted to service and the people of the Qur'an!

---

2   Ziya Paşa, the pseudonym of Abdulhamid Ziyaeddin, was an Ottoman writer, translator and administrator. He was one of the most important authors during the Tanzimat period of the Ottoman Empire. He held several offices in the State.

3   Abdullah Ibn Ubayy Ibn Salul was a prominent figure in Medina before Islam. He aspired to be the leader of Medina, but Prophet Muhammad's, peace be upon him, coming to Medina overturned his plans. He appeared to have accepted Islam, but in fact he did not. This is why he is known to be the leader of hypocrites.

Devoted to the Truth 2

Souls devoted to the Truth possess a heavenly profundity; they have abstracted themselves from physicality and pushed aside their animal side. They behold the entire existence – and, for that matter, beyond existence – through the mirror of the heart and spirit. They always feel the All-Truth in the depths of their soul. Their pulse beats with love and ardent longing for Him; their thoughts are tremulous with a concern about failing to keep their course. They maintain their humility with a sense of awe before Divine majesty. The devoted souls are distant from worldly attachments and concerns; their sole relation to the world and everything in it is with regard to seeing things as His works. They live constantly imbued with knowledge of God (*marifa*). Their attitude and state of being are permeated with awe and reverence before God's grandeur, which is so deeply ingrained in their character traits that the dwellers of heaven behold them in admiration. Actually, these are the very points that elevate them to the same level with the highest of the high, the paragons of virtue. The poet Akif put this as follows:

It is neither knowledge nor conscience that elevates character

It is reverence to God that evokes the sense of virtue in people

This profundity of their connection with Him means they constantly breathe with contentment and peace the breezes of Divine grace, and they virtually feel they are in a shelter of Providence and Guardianship all the time. In response to such sincere feelings for Him, the

Almighty Protector protects them too, as He did with the great guides of the past. The Almighty reminded the Sultan of Prophets, Muhammad, peace be upon him, of the fact that those He took under His protection are His favorite servants with the verse: *"And do not drive away any of those who solely seek God's good pleasure and call upon their Lord day and night!..."* (al-An'am 6:52).

God wishes they be guarded too, as He guards over those who devote themselves to the Truth, who present a different profundity every moment with their deep devotions and worship, whose faces are ever turned to Him, who open up to Him all the time, and who ache to gain His good pleasure.

How can it be otherwise while munificence is His comportment and being faithful is His unchanging Divine disposition? As a requirement of being fully oriented to Him, the fortunate ones who turned their backs to the pomp of both worlds are those who constantly overflow with love and sigh with longing. They lead a life in the footsteps of the Companions of Prophet Muhammad, peace be upon him—along the course of Bilal, in the clime of Habbab, in admiration of Yasir and Sumayya, and in the shade of Ibn Mas'ud. God will view those fortunate ones who turned away from both worlds accordingly, for He is the One of ultimate mercy, ultimate munificence, and ultimate compassion. If they have rooted the world out of their hearts, then the One of ultimate affection, munificence, and compassion will never leave them halfway.

In fact, besides this immense Providence and guardianship of God, there are certain prominent figures in our time, similar to those with dead hearts in the Prophet's era of light. These figures will not tolerate the mere presence of the Godly souls who have nothing to do with worldliness. They will perpetrate unheard-of atrocities against them, continually devising certain devilish projects and by trampling on law and justice to seize everything the latter has; they will commit the most wicked oppression. With a dignified resignation and self-possession like Prophet Job (Ayyub) had, devotees of service to God will dismiss it by saying, "God had given all in our possession, and God has taken them back"; thus, they will change the lane and move forward, as they are currently doing! They chose this path with an awareness of encountering such things anyway.

They knew that as it happened the unpurified souls open to evil suggestions by Satan and the carnal soul will continue to harm today, as they did yesterday. They will pester the heroes of revival who wish to uphold human and spiritual values, and they will try to destroy the most benevolent things by causing so much pain. Besides, masses of hundreds of thousands with no consciousness will participate in these efforts of the devil and his henchmen. To the shameful pages of history fouled by tyrant pharaohs, new dark pages will be added, and the cycle of historical recurrences will once more rend hearts. As it happened in the past, and will continue to do so today and tomorrow, new tyrants will come to the stage and will regard every means as fair for the sake of reaching their wicked ends; with a Machiavellian understanding, they will commit their condemned acts and will even outdo earlier tyrants. Their acts will lead to concentric, vicious circles of problems, and, thus, humanity will once more go through an era of pharaohs and oppressors.

What falls on the heroes of revival before this set of alarming pictures is to proceed in the direction of their own horizons and leave everything to the extra and special graces of God, in compliance with the Divine statements that indicate His Guardianship: *"So leave them plunging about in play and amusement until the Day (of Judgment) which they have been promised"* (az-Zukhruf 43:83; al-Ma'arij 70:42); or *"So leave them to Me..."* (al-Qalam 68:44).

Let the others keep walking on zigzagging dust paths – resolute heroes of the path of Truth should run to eliminate obstacles between every human and God, and help them open their consciences to Him, for their consciences are where His Self-Disclosure occurs. And they should put an end to the few-centuries-long separation from Him. It is in this way that essential rights and freedoms will become an indispensable factor for the public conscience. Breezes of love and respect will start to blow everywhere, and dissension and discord will come to an end. Ways leading to an ideal social, economic, and administrative structure as pictured in utopias will be opened, and the whole land will gain a condition that is enviable, trusted, cozy, and like Paradise. It will be like Paradise in spite of the crude souls devoid of compassion and beneficence who set war against fresh springs.

The swelling dawns of those bright days have already begun to appear. The next, one hopes, is that these dawns to be recognized and duly understood in the public conscience. A worldwide acceptance and understanding for those devoted to Truth is beginning to be seen, and this flows into unbiased bosoms as brilliant rays of light and brings relief to those who do care about tomorrow. The rest of the issue remains to how much endeavor we show to turn to God completely, not falling to stagnancy on the path being walked, and being able to comprehend events with their dimensions visible and invisible to our eyes. Once this is ensured, light will once more win over darkness. Let us end with words from the late poet Akif:

The days promised to you by God will appear,
Who knows, maybe tomorrow, or maybe even sooner!

DEVOTED TO THE TRUTH 3

The devoted to the Truth is a caravan of faith and perfect goodness. They walk forward free from their own shadows, facing the sun. They see the light and dark for what they are in that brightness. They do not give in to deviation and disappointment as they bypass probable lapses thanks to spotlights of perfect goodness (*ihsan*). They do not go astray, as some corrupt ones have, and with the petition *"guide us to the Straight Path"* (al-Fatiha 1:6) on their tongue, they move forward to the beyond, and even further. Although the roads are relentless, and road bandits are ruthless, and a different devilish trap awaits at every corner, they walk on towards their ideals taking the circumstances into consideration – even when they rest, they are active with contemplation and deep thinking.

The devoted to the Truth are so hopeful to reach the peaceful shores and meet beloved friends that they do not feel tired at all as they keep flapping wings without a break during such a constant journey. While their hearts beat with the excitement of meeting the faithful beloved, they do not neglect to extend a helping hand to those who remain halfway and are overcome by their carnal soul and material desires.

Prophet Muhammad, peace be upon him had returned from his Ascension (Mi'raj) to help others reach those horizons too. In the footsteps of this exemplary guide, those devoted to the Truth always whisper to others about the magic of turning to God and for this purpose they keep running breathlessly like a noble steed. And they should: because we are going through dark days; humanity has lost its direction, strayed to dusty paths and abandoned the main road. It has crashed head-on and suffers from the dizziness of being devoid of ideals, and continually runs in vain under the influence of devilish impulses. In such a time, they should (and they did) dedicate their souls for the sake of this cause as apostles of a revival.

There are so many losers who remain halfway on the road. They are expecting both a helping hand and a prescription to strengthen their immune system: a prescription that consists of faith, knowledge of God, love for Him, and ardent longing for reunion with Him. Those devoted to the Truth are always running with the very feeling and excitement of doing this and exerting themselves for this sake.

Their striving endeavors are not wasted; hundreds of thousands have pulled themselves together thanks to their breaths and came back to the right course of humanity with a fresh start. This way, breezes of love and acceptance blow all around; they are welcomed with sincere love across the globe. They are favored by Divine Providence, and this is because they do not ascribe their achievements to themselves but attribute those to the Divine will, to His grace and extra manifestations of His immense mercy. They believe that all of those achievements are Divine bestowals for their considerations of sincerity, resignation, and ardent longing for reunion with God. In this respect they always yearn for God calling out to Him "You, only You!" and recite the lines:

> *Can one who seeks the Beloved care about their own soul?*
> *Can one caring for their own soul be concerned for the Beloved?*
> *We hit the road immersed in Your love,*
> *We don't need anything but You; would else befit honor at all?*

Sayyid Nigari

Thus, by totally abstracting themselves from considerations other than the Divine, they view the world and everything in it through an otherworldly lens, and they vow that they will not be "bought" out of this path. Palaces, mansions, fleets of wealth, you name it; nothing can blur their eyes. While orienting themselves to otherworldliness, they do not neglect fulfilling the requirement of causes in this world. They believe compliance with requirements of causality to be a form of prayer in practice. In their perspective these two seemingly different dimensions (causality and prayer) merge to become one abundant waterfall and constantly inspire different things about the immediate world and the realm beyond (*malakut*).

Sadly, along with such harmony of intertwined goodness, some negative grunts are also heard. From time to time, the devil and his henchmen try to instigate sedition. They are now calling murderers whom they applauded as heroes of revival before, and they have even made plots to destroy them. However, these negativities are neither the first nor will be the last. From past to present, their equivalents have been there all along. And these will continue with nuances brought by differences in era.

Actually, from the beginning there have always been those who stagger their way on versus those who walk uprightly; those who follow the Straight Path (*al-sirat al-mustakim*) and keep their course versus those who creep lawlessly; those who respond with rectitude to being blessed with the best pattern of creation (*ahsan al-taqwim*) versus those who spend their lives with beastly urges; those who go alongside with dwellers of the heavens versus those who fall down by giving in to Satan and the carnal soul; those who always live with God's pleasure in their minds versus those who drift from one deviation to another.

These two have always existed and will always exist. However, God Almighty has never abandoned those who care for sincerity, His good pleasure, and yearn for reunion with Him. From time to time God set objectives by means of His Messengers and shed light on the horizons of journeyers to Him. And sometimes, by means of the light of the conscience, He made them remember the Primordial Covenant of their acceptance of His Lordship. Occasionally, He enforced blessings in disguise as extra signposts and always directed people to Himself. All of these have happened until today and will keep happening after today as well, by an exclusive will of God.

There will be modern versions of the Age of Ignorance. Worlds will echo with sounds of tyrants and laments of the oppressed; from time to time, there will be devils coming to the stage disguised as angels. There will arise Korahs who will cause destruction everywhere using the messages of Aaron. Corrupters misguiding the masses with the illusions of

Samiri[1] will take charge. And against the souls devoted to God on the one hand, new Amenhoteps, Cesars, Lenins, Hitlers and many modern versions of old tyrants will emerge.

Conversely, sincere journeyers of the path of the Prophets will never cease to exist either. Without any lapses, they will always ache for gaining God's good pleasure, and they will call people to abandon different forms of slavery and gain freedom by being a servant to God only. They will call others as Prophets called their people: *"O my people! Worship God alone: you have no deity other than Him!"* (al-A'raf 7:59, 65, 73, 85; Hud 11:50, 61, 84; al-Mu'minun 23:23, 32). Thus, they will care not for the deliverance of themselves only but of others, too, and for people's awakening to the truth. They will keep up this faithful stance until their final breath and until their heart stops beating. They have set forth to call everybody to being human in the true sense and to awaken hearts to God. They set out knowing that walking on this path is hard and that the devil and his henchmen will accost them at every corner with a different conspiracy and will corrupt some with a weak character.

However, they are resolved to walk on the path of the Prophets against all odds, because when they have taken this path in the name of God, they said like Said Nursi did, that they have no love for Paradise, nor a fear of Hell; for the sake of guiding humanity to being human in the true sense, they are ready to be thrown to the fire when necessary, like Prophet Abraham, the Friend of God.

The only ideal they cherish is saving truth from assaults of falsehood, letting the whole of humanity embrace as brothers and sisters, and establishing feelings of faithfulness and accord in hearts. They know that malicious souls will not remain inactive while they walk on the path of realizing this lofty ideal. Therefore, they are not surprised at all when they witness the endeavor of certain unfortunate ones fixed on falsehood to destroy the roads and bridges in every way possible. They keep on kindling the candles of others. They have full conviction that these candles cannot be extinguished, for Divine Providence and Will are behind this issue. In this regard, they virtually keep reciting the lines:

---

[1]   Samiri is mentioned in the Qur'an (Ta-Ha 20:85 and elsewhere) as the person who built a golden statue of a calf and tried to urge the Children of Israel to worship it.

What God decreed cannot be reversed by force,

A candle He kindled cannot be extinguished by blowing of course!

Ziya Paşa

And by kindling new candles, they always walk on the path of the Prophets. May their road be clear!

POISONING OF SPIRIT

The spirit constitutes human's deepest otherworldly aspect, open to the heavens. It is like a mysterious wing that helps one remain human while also extending to the realms further beyond this one. Realizing the peak of one's human potential is a Divine grace promised when that wing is alive and spiritually alert. Its paralysis, however, means paralysis of our spiritual anatomy, which we briefly refer to as "poisoning of spirit."

Treating the poisoning of spirit is rather difficult, and in some cases, nearly impossible, for most of the time one does not feel aches and pains, nor does he or she wish to visit a physician for it. Therefore, such a person is almost like the dead, at least in the heart and spirit. Worst of all, they fail to realize the gravity of the issue. In spite of undergoing deformations in their inner world, the person further degrades their spirit, failing to see the dark end that awaits. One fails to see the true nature of things, for they are being poisoned in spirit and experiencing a blindness of insight. They cannot make sense of what they claim to be seeing. How can they make sense when their system of cognition is paralyzed, spiritual anatomy is broken, reasoning and judgment fail to function? Consequently, their abilities of cognition and discernment incapacitated with the poison, they fail to soundly judge what happens, to tell right from wrong. And as for the antidote to this poison, they see the poison again, and like one attempting to quench thirst with sea water, they burn further as they drink and continue to drink as they burn.

Factors that poison a human's spirit are too many to count. Even only one of these bears the potential to make one lose their human character. When a few of them are found together, it becomes an incurable disease, like arrogance, pride, boastfulness, seeking fame, passion for status, desire for applause and appreciation, ambition for amassing wealth, captivity to the carnal soul and its fancies, weakness for selfish interests, and upstart insolence. Those who are prone to these diseases behave so erratic due to their egotism, ostentation, spoiled behaviors, and arrogance that they drift toward a waterfall of egocentrism. Unless graced with Providential help, they will not reach safe shores or convenient ports. Instead, they end up in the whirlpools where Nimrod, the pharaohs, and their likes perished. They fail to foresee and sense the disastrous end when they will be remembered as the accursed ones.

Impoverished in thought, poisoned in spirit, and paralyzed in reasoning and judgment, such persons lead a life under the influence of animal pleasures and the drives of carnal desires; deviants who abandoned the feeling of righteousness for worldly pomp. They are blind, deaf, and heartless who have preferred transient enjoyments to the eternal bliss of the Hereafter and good pleasure of God. They are senseless ones who fail to see tomorrow, under the impulses of their animal passions. A relevant Qur'anic verse (Al 'Imran 3:14) describes such a person as one enchanted with passionate love for women, children, (hoarded) treasures of gold and silver, branded horses—and their contemporary counterparts—armored luxury cars and further worldly pomp and splendor. Under the influence of such mean things, they become unable to see the dizzying enjoyments of the Hereafter and the blissful end promised by God.

If the viral areas of one's spiritual life are vulnerable to material and carnal desires, such a person's conscience will inevitably perish. This most important dynamic of humankind is meant to flourish with God-consciousness and the ensuing awe; but when it is paralyzed, such persons cannot make sense of themselves and cannot understand the immense purpose behind the blessing of being created with "the best of stature." They cannot see the dizzying human anatomy as an index of all realms and forms of existence. They cannot correctly determine their place in the universe. They are sometimes even taken by the whirlpool of causality and start humming tunes of naturalism. Sometimes, under

the influence of impossible theories, they sing of materialism. And sometimes they take on a guise of religiosity, which is actually in conflict with
the spirit of true faith. They outwardly impersonate a believer, which
presents a hypocritical form of behavior, and, in my opinion, one more
dangerous than any other deviation.

A poisoned spirit continually goes through interwoven miseries
and sufferings. He or she is always restless with apprehensions of losing
what they have obtained. With the ambitions of keeping things in their
possession and adding more, this person runs from one worldly objec-
tive to the next. And from time to time, they are delirious with delusions
of immortality. When their mind trips over impossibilities, then they begin to wheeze with fear of death. And in almost all of these episodes of
thought, or rather delirious processes, they feel surrounded from all sides
by multi-layered darkness. The situation of such a person resembles that
of an unfortunate one depicted in the Qur'an. In terms of feelings and
thoughts, their state is, *"...like veils of darkness covering up an abysmal sea
down into its depths, covered up by a billow, above which is a billow, above
which is a cloud: veils of darkness piled one upon another, so that when he
stretches out his hand, he can hardly see it..."* (Nur 24:40). This is how they
always see the general state of affairs.

With successions of grievous nightmares, they feel as if in an abyss
of Hell. Such a person, who poisoned and paralyzed their spirit with vices of worldliness, resembles an inexperienced hunter out in the forest.
While seeking their preys, they shake with the fear of being prey to others and seek comfort by yelling and shouting. In fact, they are already
hunted by their passions and caprices but are not aware of that. Their
doors are shut with respect to metaphysical realms. They neither understand anything from the depths within human nature, nor do they feel
the harmonious tunes of billions of galaxies and constellations in space.
They extinguished their inner torch with the light of which things become meaningful. The splendid order and poetic beauty of phenomena,
the All-Encompassing knowledge, overwhelming power, and the manifest Divine Will underlying all things are meaningless to them. And in
this spiral of absences, they find themselves in a cycle of judgment. So,
by poisoning their soul, they also paralyze their mechanisms of seeing,
hearing, and assessing. The Qur'an depicts such people with its exquisite

style as follows: "*They have hearts with which they do not seek the essence of matters to grasp the truth, and they have eyes with which they do not see, and they have ears with which they do not hear. They are like cattle (following only their instincts) – rather, even more astray...*" (Araf 7:179).

There have been many people of this type in the past, and so will there be in the future. But there will also be those with lustrous faces who take their physicality under control, who overcome their animal side and become oriented to the life of the heart and spirit. What falls to us is letting our shadow remain behind us, walking on the Divine path with sincerity, seeking to gain God's good pleasure, and yearning to attain His presence. For it is an unchanging Divine principle that when you show your care, you will receive the same. Muhammed Lütfi Efendi voices this fact so beautifully:

> *If You truly love the Lord, do you think He will not love you?*
> *If you seek His good pleasure, will He not let you attain it?*
> *If your tears turn to a stream, if you cry like Job did*
> *If your heart truly grieves, will He not show any sympathy?*

May God Almighty bless us with that special blessing, as a grace out of His Providence.

FACING THE SELF – SELF-RECKONING

Keeping oneself under constant watch is as important as understanding oneself, seeing how our potential to goodness can be realized, and being aware of our aspects prone to evil. Otherwise, it is very difficult—maybe even impossible—to avoid lapses and to lead a life in rectitude. Failing to take the carnal soul under control may fail a person to live up to their status as "the best pattern of creation"; they can never be saved from certain undesirable attitudes and behaviors, and cannot gain insight into the fine mysteries in their nature. They cannot gain this insight as far as the carnal soul and fancies keep obscuring their view. One who falls to such blindness will continually experience eclipses in terms of the truth of existence and the "truth of truths." Such a person cannot break free from the atmosphere darkened by dependence on the carnal soul, and becomes entangled with overwhelming caprices brought by their egotistic thoughts. Their main point of reference is always themselves. This is particularly true if the cultural environment in which the person originated engenders such feelings.

The social atmosphere in our time is quite murky: masses are unaware of the purpose of creation; those who mention such a purpose do so only with affectation, or "imitative faith." What is said does not go beyond lip service and does not come from the heart. For them, sacred concepts are mere arguments implemented for the sake of worldliness. Greed for wealth, the disease of attachment to the world as if it will last forever, bohemian weaknesses, and the deliberate preference of the worldly life over eternities... This is a riddle not pondered upon.

In such a context, unfortunate masses are like walking dead, whereas those who bring them to this condition are like devils and Machiavellian hypocrites. Although on the outside they appear to be representatives of a noble cause, each of them is a pharaonic tyrant on the inside. "I have become a servant," Jalaluddin Rumi said; but these hypocrites let out pharaonic cries and regard everybody as slaves to themselves. In the places they visit, they make sanctimonious shows and sigh like a Sufi dervish; they mesmerize their listeners by always talking about God and His Messenger, but in truth they have no true connection with them in their heart. They utter their make-believe righteous discourses, they perform as dervishes, but they never do any of that with sincerity. Each of them is so worldly-minded and their points about the sacred things they reference are nothing for them but disposable arguments to serve their own sanctimony. In the words of Aşık Pasha:

A genuine dervish is one who forsakes the world,

A genuine believer is one forsaken by the world.

Forsaking the world; those worshippers of the world do not have a grain of that feeling and consideration. All of their voices are but growls of deception. It is so difficult to talk about their share of faith, religion, and perfect goodness: almost all of them resemble Ibn Salul [the chief hypocrite during the Prophet's time]. Their world of thoughts is foul, their behaviors are pretense, the ideal they seek is pomp and magnificence, and all they want to obtain is the world and everything it offers. They give great importance to outward appearance, and wear makeup all the time. They try to fascinate those around them with embellished statements. Desperate to hide their dirty affairs they resort to all forms of demagogy to always appear white-washed. When their vices are revealed, they manufacture artificial news to cover them up. They do not know about purity of the heart and spirit; they deceive incognizant masses with their outwardly faithful appearance and let them follow behind. They always mention how they are heroes of truth and revival, but they have no relation with the truth nor pursue any effort for revival. Their feelings and thoughts are corrupt. They do not know that integrity is essential, that they should be sincere servants to God by breaking free from the commands of the carnal soul and fancies.

Considering their mechanism of conscience, their willpower and determination is faltering. Every state of theirs is deceptive with their pretense of worship. They seem to be taking ablutions and walk to the first rank as if they would observe the prayer, but all of their acts are make-believe. Their standing and sitting at prayer are all deception. They do not know the consciousness of being seen by God (*ihsan*); they pollute the means of ascension to God with their foul minds and spirits. Their inner worlds are not purified from the filth of affectation and sanctimony. However, servitude and prayer (*salah*), which is a believer's ascension (*mi'raj*), can be real only after such purification. İsmail Hakkı Bursevi puts this so well:

Purify your soul from the dirt of fancies,
Do not consider cleanliness as a mere washing of hands and face!

The unfortunate ones who cannot liberate themselves from the decoys of the carnal soul cannot be saved from leading a wavering life. They cannot give any consideration about what will happen tomorrow, what will happen further beyond, and about the Day of Judgment when they will be brought to account for everything they did in this world. Their conscience is closed against the principle, "Reckon with yourself before you are reckoned with at that great tribunal"[1] (Umar ibn al-Khattab). They are not aware that this is the only way through which they can walk to the horizons of being human in the true sense. They are not aware that only with such spiritual vigilance will it be possible to curb the carnal soul and overcome their animal desires. However, these souls poisoned with giving themselves up to worldly ranks, fame, glory, status, luxury, and applause cannot even realize that they are sailing towards such a whirlpool. They cannot know about real faith (*iman*), Islam, and perfect goodness (*ihsan*), and they cannot truly feel the immensity in being human. How can they, while they dedicate themselves entirely to worldliness with their hearts, minds, eyes, and ears, as some unfortunate ones without tomorrows?

---

1   Tirmidhi, *Qiyama*, 25; Ibnu'l-Mubarak, *Zuhd*, 1:103; Ibn Abi Shayba, *al-Musannaf*, 7/96.

However, if we do not, and cannot, see the present world and transient things as superficial but totally turn to tomorrows and beyond with the entirety of our faculties and systems of feeling, then we might fall to a position of committing disrespect against our being blessed with the best pattern of creation and charged with ingratitude to God. On the other hand, no matter what we say, it is unavoidable for souls not oriented to God to be entangled by goading of the devil and carnal soul. Imam Shafi says, "if you do not busy yourself with righteous pursuits, then futile things and falsehood will capture your soul and will keep you busy." This is an important prescription entrusted to our consciences.

***

Facing oneself seriously and leading a life in accordance with the principle, "Reckon with yourself before you are reckoned with at that great tribunal," depends on taking a resolute stance against the carnal soul and fancies and nullifying one's ego with the conviction that absolute infinity belongs to God.

This is what falls to the human as a being who is impotent, poor, needy, and whose everything is entrusted by Him. For one who keeps saying "I," vistas for seeing the truth will completely be shut, and all sides will turn into a dungeon and turn pitch dark. A person of a vigilant heart and spirit voices this point so well:

> *You do not manifest Yourself while I am appearing on the screen;*
>
> *The condition for Your self-disclosure is my self-effacement*
>
> Gavsi

Even if they are in a high spiritual state of immersion (*istighraq*) and stupor (*hayman*), all doors to the beyond will be closed to the one who keeps saying "I" and they will start experiencing ordeals, which, as a matter of fact, are meant to turn them to the righteous path. Such unfortunate ones who do not acknowledge themselves to be nil before the Infinite are subjected to Divinely enforced nullification – it is as in math when the product of two negative integers is always positive; or when *non-existence* does not exist, then there is *existence*. Likewise, when one does not acknowledge their impotence and poverty, they drift away in a flood of non-existence and cannot return.

This is the situation of the human vis-à-vis God Almighty as His servant. To the degree of feeling one's nothingness in the conscience it becomes possible to extend oneself to the horizons of knowledge of God (*marifatullah*), love for God (*mahabbatullah*), and spiritual pleasures, as a result of which one becomes a bright mirror for the Truth. Otherwise, when a person grows arrogant and starts booming with pride and conceit, then they experience concentric eclipses and become a plaything for Satan. In order not to fall into such grievous situations, one must abandon what should be abandoned, and take on what must be taken on. Choices in life must be made in accordance with Divine teachings so as not to regret in the near or distant future. İbrahim Hakkı of Erzurum summarizes this point as follows:

> *Eat little, sleep little, and drink little…*
>
> *Forsake the swamp of carnality!*
>
> *Migrate to the rose garden of the heart.*
>
> …
>
> *What God will do, let's wait and see*
>
> *Surely beautiful it will be.*

Emir Buhari of Bursa says:

> *The path of the Naqshbandi[2] requires one to renounce four things:*
>
> *Renounce the world, renounce the Hereafter,*
>
> *renounce one's existence, renounce the act of renouncing.*

This is a counsel for completely turning to God, by means of renouncing—in terms of the carnal soul—this world, [the gains and pleasures in the] next world, oneself, and even the thought of having renounced everything for the sake of God. While he mentions such hard criteria for their path, Said Nursi, as the spokesperson of his age, offers a new perspective with an emphasis on acknowledging human powerlessness and poverty, being zestful and thankful, and exercising compassion and contemplation:

2   One major Sufi order.

The path of powerless ones requires one (to acknowledge) four things:
Absolute poverty, absolute powerlessness,
absolute thankfulness, and absolute zest, O dear friend!

Every word uttered for the sake of reading ourselves correctly, for self-reckoning, and determining our position before God is a precious statement, even though they are from different perspectives, as expressed by Muhibbi:

For some, the beloved stood as elegant as a cypress
For others, as graceful as the letter alif,
Their descriptions are different, but they all mean the same

It is thanks to such statements that the heart keeps up its life with considerations of *ihsan*, i.e., perfect goodness, and becomes illuminated. It is how one can keep up his or her position before God. Thus, the person frequently exercises self-analyses on this path. They realize a correct self-reading of both their own tainted and shining aspects with exercises of self-purification. Busy with their own self-purification, the person does not see the dirt and grime of others; even if they see they would mind their own business. Sometimes such a person sighs like Niyazi Mısri, who said:

I did not have a wise trade, my lifetime capital is gone wasted,
I came to the road, but the entire caravan had moved away, unaware;
I cried, lamented and took the road lonely.
The eye cries, the bosom burns, the mind overwhelmed, unaware.

Sometimes with the sincerity of the poet Leyla Hanım, one exercises severe self-criticism:

I fell for the fancies of my soul, and committed so many sins,
O Messenger of God! How can I have the face to come to your presence?

Sometimes with the depth of the Imam of Alvar (M. Lütfi Efendi), one can sadly open up to God and say:

> *Neither do I have knowledge nor good deeds,*
> *Nor do I have any power for goodness,*
> *Immersed in rebellions, with much wrongdoing,*
> *I wonder what will become of me on the Day of Reckoning.*

And so many more have opened up to God in this regard with the consideration of "facing the self."

Let us conclude for now with these monumental personages who ran from one degree of self-reckoning and repentance to another and direct our attention in the following articles to the situation of perfected ones, with the following truth in our minds:

"The good deeds of the righteous ones (*abrar*) can be considered sin for those nearest to God (*muqarrabin*)."[3]

Help and success are from God.

Ajluni, *Kashfu'l-Khafa*, 1/428.

FACING THE SELF – EMBODIMENTS OF RECTITUDE

E*mbodiments of rectitude* are exceptional people who look at life with a holistic view. They see things correctly, they think correctly, and they attach their every initiative with a consideration for truth. They move forward between the carnal soul and what lies beyond their nature always with this consideration in mind. They turn the lens of their willpower and consciousness to behold their inner world and check with their essential nature; then they turn it to beyond and even further beyond to open up to the Creator. They give an account of their situation to Him, renew their covenant, and humbly prostrate themselves. They are aware of the fact that they are mirrors to the Divine and that they are created as an index for all existence and the universe.

With such an all-comprehensive awareness, these people always endeavor to act in accordance with the purpose of their creation and frequently supervise their inner worlds. They come to grips with themselves and keep vigilant against contamination of their considerations. They live with an alertness to not allow any darkening of the heart and rusting of the spirit. Most of the time, with a concern for having contaminated them, they run to purifying basins of turning to God, and they constantly sigh with the thought that they failed to give the due of the honor of being the best of creation.

They never open the door of their imagination to any form of filth; let alone that, they shake like a leaf fearing the possibility of the least contamination of their dreams or conceptions and fog of stagnancy. In the face of such a possibility, they start seeking fresh means of turning to

55

God. Their hands always on the knob of Divine mercy and forgiveness, they lead an angelic life. Given that they are heroes of closeness to God and are burning with a love for reunion with Him, then their way should be the lane of ardent longing for reunion with God. This should be the staircase of overcoming one's own remoteness and attaining togetherness beyond forms with the One Who is closer than the closest to us!

Those who did reach the horizons did so with such resolution and great effort; as for those entangled by the web of their fancies, however, they remained halfway on the road. Throughout history, those who took their shadow behind them and always walked with their face turned to the sun reckoned and came to grips with themselves with depth. They trembled with concerns for falling on account of things they saw, or rather assumed they saw, in their hearts, spirit, conceptualizations, and imaginations. As their feelings, excitement and worries were reflected in their words, they kept sighing and sincerely implored God Almighty.

From Prophet Muhammad – the brilliant moon, peace be upon him – to the stars that gathered around his perfect guidance, all of the embodiments of rectitude have become loyal journeyers on the path of the Prophets leading to a reception with the Divine, and they have presented exemplary behaviors that will never misguide later generations who follow their footsteps. May their way be clear and may the All-Merciful Lord render us journeyers of that path, too!

Now, let us try to push a door to look at Prophet Muhammad, peace be upon him, who is for us the unique vanguard of this road, the most distinguished and blessed guide of all time. Let us have a vista to see his example and come to grips with ourselves, with the acknowledgement that our own situation could only be that of a drop in the ocean.

The Prophet, the blessed master of the created and who had the utmost closeness to God, would open up to Him with an expansive state of his spirit, attitude of self-possession, and a consideration of guiding those behind him; and thus, his morning was a separate session of vigilance, and his evening was a different time of turning to God. *"Glorified are You, O God!"* he would pray, and although sins did not visit him even in his dreams, he would say, *"I seek Your forgiveness for my sins, and I ask You for Your mercy."*[1]

---

1   Abu Dawud, *Adab*, 107.

Thus, the Messenger of God would show the way to exercise self-supervision to his followers and present an astounding attitude of humbleness and effacement. Likewise, when daybreak drew near, his sincere petitioning was like a wake-up call for those who heedlessly indulged themselves in sleep and an admonition to the fluctuant. He would touch the doorknob of Divine mercy by beseeching as follows:

> "I seek refuge in You from wronging others and being wronged, from committing aggression and being the object of aggression, and from committing an error or a sin which is not forgiven."[2]

He did this even though these were miles and miles away from even entering his world of imagination. How I wish if only a quarter of this opening up to God were found within us and leaders of our nations.

Even before he was a Prophet, and certainly after he was, at almost every phase of his blessed life he kept his carnal soul and fancies under control; in spite of this, he met every new sunrise with diamond words of supplication rising from his heart, in a manner of self-possession: *"My Lord, truly if you leave me to myself, You'd leave me to weakness I cannot bear, an overwhelming need, sin and error."* After these words from his vigilant soul, he would conclude his blessed appeal as follows, which befits him so well: *"Truly I rely on nothing except Your mercy, so forgive me all my sins, for no one forgives sins except You."*[3] He prayed thus as if he ever had any sins!

He continued opening up to God and against the carnal soul and Satan, who could not even visit his world of imagination. He said the following, repeating four times, which I think was actually a way of giving counsel to his followers: *"My God, I seek refuge in You from the evil of my self, the evil of Satan and his traps, and from committing wrong to myself or another believer."*[4] Such a degree of self-possession and deliberation! He would not suffice with these, holding the doorknob of mercy, Divine protection, and guardianship, he would pray as:

> "Ya Hayyu Ya Qayyum (O Giver of life and Who maintains it)! For

2   Ahmad ibn Hanbal, *al-Musnad*, 5/191; Tabarani, *al-Mu'jamu'l-kabir*, 5/119.

3   Ahmad ibn Hanbal, *al-Musnad*, 5/191; Tabarani, *ad-Dua*, p.122.

4   Tirmidhi, *Daawat*, 105; Ahmad ibn Hanbal, *al Musnad*, 2:171.

the sake of Your Mercy, I beg for help. Rectify all my states of being and leave me not to myself even for the blinking of an eye!"[5]

Let his example illuminate the blind eyes and deaf ears of those who stumble through their lives. He was so sensitive and vigilant against the carnal soul and fancies that even though he was miles away from them, they did not—could not—cast a shadow on his radiant world of thought. We take a step back again and once more give an ear to the deep sighs and petitioning of that sultan of speech: *"I seek refuge in You from the evil of my soul and from the evil of every creature in Your grasp."* What vigilance! What an immense feeling of self-possession!

Even his archenemies did not, or could not, dare ascribe the least degree of vice to him. Both before his mission as the Messenger of God and afterwards, he was acknowledged by all as the most trustworthy person. Yet, as if he had any shortcomings, he would pray, *"O God! Conceal my imperfections and calm all my fears!"*[6] How exalted he is! He certainly did not have any shortcomings, but let us take this prayer as our guide counseling us, for we are the ones who need guidance.

In terms of his considerations of awe and reverence before Divine grandeur, he had a heart that always shook with fear of God. In this respect, he was marking the course leading to true virtue for those to follow his way. Saying that he would sleep at night like we do is gross disrespect against him, because he had settled this issue, too, by stating *"my eyes do sleep, but my heart does not."*[7] However, even when that distinguished soul who surpassed angels was to enter his special sleep, he would earnestly turn to God wholeheartedly and say:

> "O God! in Your name have I laid down on my side. Forgive me my sins and drive away my devil; release me from my dependency (on others) and place me in the highest assembly!"[8]

In spite of his much lauded and distinguished position, he was teaching so much to us even with that deep sigh. His Ascension to the

5   Abu Dawud, *Adab*, 101; Ahmad ibn Hanbal, *al-Musnad*, 5/42.
6   Abu Dawud, *Adab*, 100; Ahmad ibn Hanbal, *al-Musnad*, 2:25.
7   Bukhari, *Tahajjud*, 16, Tarawikh 1; Muslim, *Salatu'l-Musafirin*, 125.
8   Abu Dawud, *Adab*, 107; Tabarani, *Mu'jamu'l-kabir*, 22/298.

heavens (*Mi'raj*) was blessed with the gift of daily prayers (*salah*), and his prayers were each like a new Ascension.[9] While he was heading to perform his prayers, which is like an earthly ascension, he would be imbued with perfect goodness (*ihsan*) in all of his attitudes; and when he started the worship at God's beck and call, the following blessed words would come out of his lips as a beautiful expression of the deed being observed:

> "O God, You are the Owner, there is no deity other than You. You are my sole Lord, and I am your servant. I have wronged my soul; I confess my sin. Please forgive all of my sins; no one but You can forgive them. Guide me to good character, as only You can grant guidance!"[10]

My dearest innocent soul, which sin are you talking about! These prayers are meant to call us, too, to those horizons. May God also bless us with that complete guidance. His distance, from what he mentioned as "sin," was further away from the distance between East and West, but against things he considered wrong—wrongs that did not even visit his dreams—he opened up to God and sighed with utter self-possession and a vow of perfect goodness:

> "O God, distance me from my misdeeds as You have distanced the East from the West! O God, wash away my sins with pure water, snow, and hail!"[11]

What a profundity it is, my dearest beloved one! You are the one poets praised as:

> *You are the glorified sultan of the Prophets, my master*
> *You are a majestic bestowal to helpless ones, my master*
> *You are the chief in the Divine Council, my master*

---

9   One of the major miracles of Prophet Muhammad, peace be upon him, was his journey from Mecca to Jerusalem, and from there to the heavens. In this miraculous journey into heavenly dimensions, he met with other Prophets and eventually God. One of the gifts of this journey is daily prayers (salah), which Muslims are commanded to observe five times a day.

10   Muslim, *Salatu'l-musafirin*, 201; Abu Dawud, *Salat*, 124.

11   Bukhari, *Adhan*, 89; Muslim, *Masajid*, 147.

You are the one affirmed by God's oath by your life, my master.

Şeyh Galib

Oh, the light of my endeavor and my shining sun, you are speaking in the first person and imploring God; yet, by doing so, if you are calling us to be ourselves on your blessed path, we have been alienated to those horizons with our degenerates and leaders. That being the case, our dreams are filled with hopes, and we are expecting your favor upon us; for the sake of God, do not make us wait further!

Just as you looked at those in your special circle,
Please grant a look at this humble one also,
And let me burn ablaze with your sacred love.
Let my atmosphere not be darkened with the sadness of being without you,
Please say, "he is also from me," so that I do not remain distant from you.

F. Gülen

Prostration is when a person is closest to God,[12] said the Prophet. Prostration is a unique state of being, as described in the following couplet:

Where the head meets the feet, kissing the prayer rug on the ground
This is the road that carries a person to closeness to God.

F. Gülen

The Prophet always put his head on the ground very humbly, his blessed head that never bowed before anyone other than the Almighty, and he would open up to God as follows:

"My God, please forgive all my sins. O God, forgive me for all my sins, the major and the minor, the first and the last, and the openly known and those kept secret!"[13]

My innocent sultan of sultans, your Lord did not let you commit

---

12   Muslim, *Salat*, 215; Abu Dawud, *Salat*, 148; Nasai, *Mawaqit*, 35, *Tatbiq*, 78.

13   Muslim, *Salatu'l-musafirin*, 201; Abu Dawud, *Salat*, 118; Tirmidhi, *Daawat*, 32.

sins in the past, and He sealed with your loyalty all doors and windows that lead to sin.[14] If only those who spend their lives in the filth of sins could also understand these moans and sighs loftier than breaths of angels! Unfortunately, those who said farewell to a life centered on realizing the heart's potential are unaware of the horizons of the spirit and will neither feel nor understand these sighs.

As he knelt down during his prayer (*tashahhud*) where he felt to the core his closeness to God and realized peak spiritual delight, he sighed again to the profundity of his own knowledge of God and showed how unreachable his spirit is with the following words from his heart, which are in fact meant to be reminders for unknowing ones like ourselves:

> "O God, truly I have greatly wronged my soul, and no one forgives sins except You, so forgive me with Your forgiveness, and have mercy on me, for You are the All-Forgiving, the All-Compassionate."[15]

If only we could also sigh wholeheartedly for our lagging so far behind that guide, the Messenger of God who would always woe for certain heart-darkening conditions, which might hold true for us any time and, yet, were so far away from his horizon:

> "O God, I take refuge in You from a hard heart, heedlessness, poverty, humiliation, and deprivation. I take refuge in You from want, unbelief, immorality, divisiveness, pretentiousness, and ostentation..."[16]

I don't know whether such a degree of vigilance and sobriety is ever felt by anyone else in such an astounding profundity. I do not think so and nobody else can deem it possible...

At the end of our discussed topic, which is like a drop from the ocean in terms of the Messenger's imploring and petitioning, I say, the subject is not over yet; also to be covered are the purest souls from his circle. And I beg forgiveness from God on account of my mistakes.

14   In reference to the verse, "That God may forgive you (O Messenger) your lapses of the past and those to follow, and complete His favor on you, and guide you on a straight path" (al-Fath 48:2).

15   Bukhari, *Adhan*, 151, *Daawat*, 17, *Tawhid*, 9; Muslim, *Dhikr*, 48.

16   Ibn Hibban, *Sahih*, 3/300; Hakim, *al-Mustadrak*, 1/712.

FACING THE SELF – PROPHETIC HORIZONS

It is beyond our horizon to evaluate the Prophets' relationship with God, the way they self-reckoned, and how touching and self-possessed their grief were at the gates of the Divine despite their innocence. Their otherworldly profundity as well as their feelings of awe and reverence before God cannot be contained by volumes. The same goes for their imploring petitions and heart-rending supplications presented to the beyond and even further. Our expressions are a drop compared to the ocean, or a photon compared to the light of a full moon. How can we put into words how the Prophets, who were purified with Divine mercy from the beginning, ran from one basin of purification to another? But still, I believe in the necessity of this effort and thus will dare to make some comments in this matter, hoping that looking at their example will help us gather ourselves together and come to our senses. May God Almighty grant us a drop of their lofty feelings!

Prophet Muhammad (peace be upon him)

In the diamond succession of the Prophets, the first "facing the self" took place in the form of heartfelt sighs and sobs of Prophet Adam, peace be upon him. This happened as a result of what is called a "lapse," which was but a nonviable judgment on when the time of *breaking the fast*, so to speak, would be. I am purposefully avoiding the word "mistake"; this is to be covered later on hopefully. We need to note down here that the words God Almighty uses about His servants are always welcome as exclusive to the Lord and His servants; it is not our job to pass judgments

63

on God's messengers, and we should always think and speak with caution about these "chosen, righteous ones" (Saad 38:47).

Although "facing the self" in the Prophetic horizons started with Prophet Adam (as briefly referred to in the above paragraph) and simple logic expects us to begin with him, the pure servant of God and the first Prophet, our heart rather tends to start off beautifully with the last one, Prophet Muhammad, peace and blessings be upon him, who was the raison d'être of the universe, who came last but took the lead even before those in the fore.

Prophet Muhammad, peace be upon him, is the opener of the secret wisdom of the world. He is the first one who existed in Divine knowledge before all,[1] the crown of all dwellers of the earth and heavens, the one who came with universal messages to be a guide for the entire humanity: the pride of dwellers of the earth and heavens, that matchless Sultan of the Prophets, known among both spirit and physical beings as the Creator's prime locus of attention, who pours the rays of Divine light and inspirations from beyond into those hearts that are open to faith, and who bears the title of the greatest spiritual pole of all of the physical and metaphysical realms. In terms of his Prophetic qualities of innocence, purity, trustworthiness, loyalty, intellect, and communicating the message, Muhammad, the Messenger of God, is even beyond all distinguished ones. A saintly poet describes him as follows:

> *This world is a mirror, and everything stands with the Divine,*
>
> *In the mirror of Muhammad, God is reflected all the time.*
>
> (*Aziz Mahmud Hudayi*)

The honorable Messenger is regarded by anyone unbiased as a remarkable explorer of the truths of Uniqueness (*ahadiyya*) and Self-Sufficiency (*samadiyya*) of the One Whom all depend on. He is appreciated in the utmost degree as the most eloquent expresser of the Truth of truths. Despite all these qualities, he always walked on the path of modesty and

1   For Muslims, Prophet Muhammad, peace be upon him, is the best of humankind, thus the ultimate fruit of the tree of creation. Seed is the first form of existence before the tree's branches and leaves, and the fruit of a tree is encoded in that seed. Likewise, the Prophet is considered to be the first among all creation.

humbleness. He was a hero of altruism, for he came back to the world from his heavenly Ascension (*mi'raj*) when he bid a temporary farewell to the holiest reunion with God to be able to teach everyone about the Truth. So, in the name of God we would like to begin with that example who was superior to angels, who was a matchless paragon of virtue.

We cannot help but wonder why Prophet Muhammad, peace be upon him, implored God and wailed so much despite all of his virtues and inner profundity and being so innocent. He always led a life centered on deep devotion to God with a consciousness of perfect goodness (*ihsan*) as broadly outlined below.

Although he came last in terms of corporeal existence among the Prophets, he was always on the fore and was the pioneer. Though the ode of the Prophets was structured and composed with his name, he was placed at the end of this sacred verse like a rhyme, with his conclusive universal mission.

While he was the first in one sense, he was the last in another sense. Above all, in terms of his existence in the form of pure blessed light [before he came to the physical world], he had the honor of being the first: "The first of what God created was my light."[2] By implication to this meaning, he also said: "*I was a Prophet while Adam was between water and clay,*"[3] and thus referred to this puzzle of being the first and the last. With reference to this mysterious seniority, we would like to begin covering this diamond succession with him, that noblest soul ever oriented to God.

The Prophet never allowed mistaken things to enter his life, even in his imaginations or dreams. Sleep is regarded as the sister of death, but in his case, it was all about closing his eyes, while his heart remained vigilant. When that noble soul would retire to sleep, however, he would never sleep without reciting them first:

> *Our Lord! Take us not to task if we forget or make mistakes. Our Lord, lay not on us a burden such as You laid on those gone before us. Our Lord, impose not on us what we do not have the power to bear. And*

2   See al-Suyuti, *al-Hawi*, 1/325; al-Halabi, *al-Siratu'l-Halabiyya*, 1/240.

3   al-Sahawi, *al-Maqasidu'l-hasana*, p. 522; Aliyyu'l Qari, *al-Asraru'l-marfua*, p. 271; al-Ajluni, *Khashfu'l Khafa*, 2/173. 60

overlook our faults, and forgive us, and have mercy upon us. You are
our Guardian and helper, so help us and grant us victory against the
disbelieving people! (al-Baqara 2:286)

O the exalted and pure soul! You did not have anything to do with
mistakes. If this petition of yours is a counsel for degenerates in need of
guidance like myself, then we say, "We have heard and obeyed,"[4] by taking your petitions in the sense of showing us the way, and we respectfully
salute your being of pure blessed light. Otherwise, if you stated them with
reference to yourself, then we close our eyes and ears to be immersed in
silent self-supervision; this, because even your relentless enemies would
call you "the Trustworthy" (*al-Amin*) when they were simmering with
grudge and hatred. They would hold their tongue when they encoun-
tered your innocence and decency, and would at least temporarily stop
their grunting. If only I could make my voice be heard to your highness,
O beloved one, but my rebellious nature does not allow that! Tell me for
God's sake, are your pains and opening up to God with such manifold
self-possession a secret that belongs to those closest to God, or are they
allusive orders for miserable ones like us?

I wonder what lay behind the Prophet's immense consideration
and punctiliousness. This should have been in line with the Divine address that states what needs to be stated:

> *Surely, We have sent down to you the Book with the truth (embodying*
> *it, with nothing false in it), so that you should judge between people*
> *according to how God has shown you. So do not be a pleader on behalf*
> *of those who betray their trust. Pray God for forgiveness, as God is*
> *All-Forgiving, All-Compassionate.* (an-Nisa 4-105-106)

These two verses sound more like addressing the followers of the
Prophet than himself, for he was never likely to act in the way as mentioned. However, this Divine decree had resonated like the deep cry of
a reed flute in his exquisitely fine and sensitive soul. With the sensitivity
of his blessed soul, he doubtlessly took the message directly upon him as
it happened when he said that the Chapter Hud (verse 112) made him

4   Al-Baqara 2:285; an-Nisa 4:46; al-Ma'ida 5:7; an-Nur 24:51.

old[5] with the command, *"Pursue, then, what is exactly right, as you are commanded (by God)."*

O the Prophet, the exalted soul! May all souls be your ransom! Your blessed life passed much beyond mere rectitude, always with awe and reverence before God; however, you took that Divine decree as if it were referring to you and suffered for it. We are the ones being addressed; but we have failed to understand and failed to burn inside as you did. If only we could understand that each of us is responsible for things commanded in address to you. It is such a bitter reality that we have lived so heedlessly; we have never been able to give our status its due.

O the Pride of Humanity, and the unique one of all space and times! Pardon us, we have kept claiming to be your followers, but we have unfortunately fallen far behind and wasted our lives virtually crawling both in living our faith and in being its true exemplars. When you turn to your eternal Lord, please petition like you always do once more for us degenerate souls, too, and implore God that these poor souls who remained distant from Him and from you to become true believers at heart! Please pray so that God lets us also be human in the real sense of the word.

Prophet Adam (peace be upon him)

Regardless of factors like time and the nature of his existence, the life of Prophet Adam, the pure one of God (Safiyullah), peace be upon him, is one in which "facing the self," self-accounting, and relations with God go hand-in-hand. He led a life always turned to God and regarded the slightest lapse as a demotion. He never ceased to implore God with repentance and always kept a watchful gaze, both with his heart and his eyes, on the door to the Divine; he always had the remembrance of His Name on his tongue.

Prophet Adam was created from mud and "sounding" clay (ar-Rahman 55:14) to be, as it were, the womb human spirit was to be breathed into, and as a concise index of the book of universe. Honored as the point of direction for the angels' prostration, he was brought to existence as a result of the combination of this conscious spirit (*ruh*) – which is "of the Lord's command" (al-Isra' 17:85) – with matter. He was the noble and

5   Tirmidhi, *Tafsir*, (56) 6; Munawi, *Faydhu'l-Qadr*, 4/169.

esteemed father of all humanity; the distinguished kernel of the succession of the Prophets that was ready to flourish, a sapling open to bearing fruit, and a brightened mirror of God honored with *the best pattern of creation.*

Prophet Adam was a comprehensive mirror in a different dimension. He was in a position of being a key to the Hidden Treasure of the Divine (*kanzan makhfiyyan*), along with being a brilliant mirror to God's all-encompassing knowledge, overwhelming power, and supreme will. Persons of profound insight could have access to the doors of Divine doings (*af'al*), works (*asar*), names (*asma*), attributes (*sifaat*), qualities, states (*shu'unat*), and of Divine Self (*Dhaat*) by means of comprehending and analyzing Prophet Adam's physical and spiritual anatomy correctly.

Those with vigilant consciences who understand and appreciate him would always be on the road to the Truth without any fatigue; as they would try to attain knowledge of God (*marifatullah*), love for God (*mahabbatullah*), and spiritual delight, they'd move forward seeking togetherness with the One Whose existence is without comparison. In the meantime, some unfortunate ones with gaps in their hearts and prone to devilish signals would remain stuck on the roads, and so have they done.

As all children of Adam are brought to existence with seeds of angelic and satanic potentials within—their free will only as a simple cause—they sometimes take wing to the highest of the high in a way to surpass angels and sometimes remain at the lowest of the low. This occurred with great personages in the form of a lapse, whereas it also occurred with those prone to Satan in the form of serious falls. On a great or small scale, such deviations have always occurred, and will continue to occur in the future, too.

In the words of the poet Mehmet Akif, Adam's nature was "loftier than that of the angels"; in him "realms were hidden, and worlds were compacted." However, a lapse, which we can call one little stumble, was also inevitable for him but never to adulterate his purity. Since this temporary lapse was a result of his reasoning effort (*ijtihad*), he was still to get one reward, not two.[6] Actually, it was a timing issue that he laid hand

6   This is based on a *hadith* by Prophet Muhammad, peace be upon him: "When a

on the forbidden fruit; he could not reckon when exactly he would be allowed to do so.[7] Still, the Almighty Lord admonished him in a way that He would do for those whom God made closest to Himself. With this, he was in fact being pushed to a ground where he would yield the best of fruits, the most blessed ones, with his special inner qualities he was not yet aware of. As M. Lütfi Efendi, the Imam of Alvar, puts it:

> *The actual wisdom behind the tree*
> *was the coming of Muhammad the blessed to this world!*

But how to explain this wisdom to Adam, the pure servant of God! His lapse grew bigger and bigger in his eyes for a lifetime, and he always suffered with the feeling of having disobeyed his Lord. Although he was among those closest to God, he lived repentantly in a mood of awe and reverence before God. He always looked down in shame for years and did not raise his head to the sky. Voicing his true feelings, he constantly said, *"Our Lord! We have wronged ourselves, and if You do not forgive us and do not have mercy on us, we will surely be among those who have lost!"* (al-A'raf 7:23). What an immense coming to grips with his soul and a scrupulous care about his relationship with God! What a profound mood of self-possession and vigilance!

Some weak narrations relate the following as an alleviation to the sufferings of his heart. Accordingly, one day Prophet Adam raised his hands and prayed, "O God please forgive me for the sake of Muhammad (peace be upon him), Your beloved!" And the response was the following relief by the Divine Providence: "How do you know him?" The pure servant of God said: "When I was sent out of Paradise, I turned back and

---

judge gives a decision, having tried his best to decide correctly and is right, there are two rewards for him; and if he gave a judgment after having tried his best (to arrive at a correct decision) but erred, there is one reward for him" (Sahih Muslim, *Book of Judicial Decisions*, 1716).

7   As in the beginning of this article (under the subheading "Prophet Muhammad, peace be upon him), the author describes Prophet Adam's situation as having made a nonviable judgment on when the time of breaking the fast would be, out of respect to the Prophetic mission and Prophet Adam's purity, peace be upon him.

looked at the gate through which I passed and there I read, 'There is no god but Allah and Muhammad is His Messenger.' Seeing the two names side by side, I inferred his esteem in Your sight and I asked forgiveness for me, for us, by means of his intercession."[8]

In his famous poem Süleyman Çelebi voices this point as follows in his imagination of God speaking to the Prophet during his Ascension:

I have taken you as a mirror to Myself;
I wrote My name and your name together.

Prophet Adam was already slated to be forgiven, and he gained it with this final invocation. I don't know whether we are properly drawing our lesson from this attitude, self-possession, and vigilance of the father of humanity who came to grips with himself even before the slightest lapse and always cried out, *"Our Lord, we have wronged our souls..."* If not, then it becomes obvious that we are poor ones with an inflicted conscience who are crushed under the weight of their carnal side.

Prophet Noah (peace be upon him)

Another one of the distinguished figures of the golden succession of the Prophets was Noah (Nuh), peace be upon him. This great personage endeavored breathlessly for so many years calling people to God and asked them to accept faith. He was subjected to insults and threats, but he constantly kept reminding them of God without giving in.

Bigots of unbelief, however, did not remain inactive; they teased him and tried to detach a handful of believers from him. But he never gave up. Contrarily, this increased his metaphysical dynamism, and he continued to fulfill his responsibility as a Prophet by communicating the message each time in a new way and with stronger resolution. As he did so, he also presented the general situation he happened to be in to God Almighty. His story is covered in different chapters of the Qur'an, including the chapter of Noah which conveys this holy chain of events very clearly. He was a person of prayer; while petitioning God with deep sighs, he worked hard with a selfless devotion to fulfilling his mission.

8   Al-Hakim, *Al-Mustadrak*, 2/615.

The Qur'an relates this feeling of Prophet Noah as follows:

> *I ask of you no wage for that (for conveying God's Message); my wage is due only from the Lord of the worlds.* (ash-Shuara 26:109)

This attitude of sincerity and dignified indifference is an indispensable quality of those on the path of the Prophets. Also known as *Najiyyullah* (the one close to God), Noah (pbuh) used his high endowments, immense insight, and Prophetic Intellect—a blessing given as an indispensable quality of God's Messengers—to call people to the Truth, and he did not cherish any expectations other than appreciation by God. Thus, he stood up to unimagined insults and never wavered in the face of unbecoming attitudes.

At the same time his mind and mouth were busy telling certain things to those around him, his heart was constantly shaking like a leaf with awe of God's majesty. On seeing that his invitations did not yield any positive results, he referred them to God, so that they would find what they would. Then with a Divine command, he set about building the ark. Never ending teasing and taunts continued all along.

In the end, the disaster bound to come did come. The great flood started with heavy rain and springs began to gush up water from underground. Many drowned, including Noah's son. With the compassion of a father, he (pbuh) petitioned to God, *"My Lord, my son was of my family (as a believer), and Your promise is surely true (for my believing family members), and You are the Most Just of judges"* (Hud 11:45).

> *"O Noah! He (being an unbeliever) is not of your family,"* God said, *"He is one of unrighteous conduct (which embodied his unbelief). So do not ask of Me what you have no knowledge of. I admonish you so that you do not behave as one among the ignorant"* (Hud 11:46).

With an attitude becoming for those closest to God like himself, he petitioned as, *"Oh my Lord! I seek refuge in You, lest I should ask of You what I have no knowledge of. And unless You forgive me and have mercy on me, I will indeed be among the losers"* (Hud 11:47). Thus, he once more turned to God in supplication with an immense self-supervision. Loyal servants at God's beck and call and monumental personages who internalized submission to Divine commands always acted this way. They always committed their affairs to God *(tafwiz)*, especially the mistakes in their judgments, feelings, thoughts, and expressions. On account of their actions and behaviors, they were self-critical and always lived as humbled with shame before God. If only we had a tenth of such sublime consideration and self-criticism!

I think if God Almighty lets our faculty of insight be open, if He bestows us the feeling of coming to grips with ourselves, then we will see how far below we are what we say and do and will be humbled with shame; unfortunately, the doors of our hearts are closed to such consciousness and comprehension; we do not see what is supposed to be seen, as much as we see ourselves. Despite our ignorance, we still regard ourselves as learned people. This is to such a degree in some people that they do not know things that need to be known, but they put on airs as if they know and look down on others. They abase not only themselves but also masses devoid of consciousness along with them. May God bestow the blessing of insight on those human-like beings who stagger their way on in the narrowness of their manifold ignorance so that they get out of animalism and corporeality, are no longer controlled by physical drives, and adopt a life centered around the heart and spirituality.

Prophet Abraham (peace be upon him)

Abraham (Ibrahim) (pbuh), the Friend of God, is another exemplar of coming to grips with himself. He has always been mentioned in the heavens and the earth with the attribute of *khulla* (sincere friendship). When Prophet Muhammad, the Pride of the Created (pbuh) was once called with this attribute, he said out of modesty and self-effacement that it belongs to Abraham (pbuh). This may be likened to a situation when the one lower in ranking is preferred in one quality over the one superior across the board – of course this is just a thought that is open to debate.

Some also understood *khulla* as perceiving the existence just like a shadow before the Glorified Existence of God, a ray of manifestation from Divine Attributes, a state of attaining a special togetherness with Him, and being regarded as a distinguished friend. A person of such horizons has nothing in their thoughts but Him. They always speak of God; when they mention "love" and "beloved," there is nothing but Him in their world of imagination beyond any forms. By looking at phenomena and events, they see the Divine Names through the lens of His works and actions. Then, they become absorbed in beholding the Divine Attributes through the telescopes of the Divine Names – eventually they cannot help but remember the Almighty.

In the sight of such a person, all beings are each a message from Him that points back to Him; and all sounds and words are like melodies crooning of Him. After gaining such a perspective, each thing and happening seems like an eloquent tongue, and the melody of those tongues is always "He." There are signs that refer to Him in every object:

> *The universe as a whole is a grand book of God,*
>
> *Try any of its letters; the meaning of each reveals nothing but Him.*
>
> Recaizade Mahmut Ekrem

With a surpassing comprehension and insight, such a spiritual journeyer experiences a constant rapture of togetherness and company with Him and never considers leaving those horizons afterwards. The way of *khulla* is journeying in a radiant atmosphere and those who are on that path are wayfarers of *khulla*, perhaps in their own relative capacity. One who adopts these attributes in the perfect sense is a *khalil* (sincere friend) in the true sense. The feelings of togetherness and love, reliance on God, and submission to Him in such a person make their presence felt in every state from the smile on their face down to all organs and limbs. Such a sincere friend repels evil with goodness and does not go eye-for-an-eye; they blow like a gentle breeze and live with a consciousness of *ihsan* (perfect goodness)—not only towards those who give positive support but even against those teeming with hatred. Such a person does not prefer to use their legitimate right to respond to evil in kind. Let alone using it, even in the face of the lowest acts of indecency, such people respond, *"So (the proper recourse for me is), a becoming patience (a patience that endures without complaint). God it is Whose help is sought against (the situation) that you have described,"* (Yusuf 12:18) and they set about waiting with active patience for how Divine fate will manifest.

These are among the indispensable ways of the horizons of *khulla*. Abraham, the friend of God, (pbuh) is a distinguished favorite of that lofty horizon. With perfect reliance on God, he was thrown to fire and endured troubles beyond imagination. He had to leave his homeland and migrate to different places. Then he rendered his migration fruitful by seeking new people to communicate his message. He virtually tried to work an embroidery of Divine oneness by shuttling between Canaan, Mecca, and Palestine. After it was destroyed, he rebuilt Ka'ba, the House of God, which is the earthly counterpart of the Lote Tree of the Furthest Limit (*Sidrat al-Muntaha*) and bequeathed it to later generations. Even while he was busy with rebuilding the Ka'ba, which was of paramount importance—together with his son Ishmael (pbuh)—he came to grips with himself in the form of petitioning God. He prayed as if he did not do anything worthwhile and oblivious of his good deeds:

> *O My Lord! Make me and those believers from my offspring observe the Prayer, and our Lord, accept my prayer! Our Lord! Forgive me, and my parents, and all the believers, on the Day on which the Reckoning will be established.* (Ibrahim 14:40-41)

Let us note here that he offered this second prayer before he was forbidden to pray for his father who made idols.

He wailed and moaned; without considering his greatness and his being honored as "the sincere friend of God," he always kept up an attitude of being ordinary. It is on account of such immense and rich qualities of his that God Almighty mentions how exemplary Abraham (pbuh) and those in his company were:

> *You have had an excellent example in Abraham and those with him, when they said to their (idolatrous) people (who were their kin): "We are quit of you and whatever you worship besides God. We have rejected you (in your polytheism), and there has arisen between us and your enmity and hate forever until you believe in God alone (as the only One to be worshipped."* (al-Mumtahina 60:4)

As their path parted from idol worshippers, as described in the above verse, they turned to God against possible evils in the future and voiced their trust in Him as follows:

> *O Our Lord! It is in You that We have put our trust, and it is to You that we turn in utmost sincerity and devotion; and to You is the homecoming. O Our Lord! Do not make us prey for those who disbelieve.*

And forgive us, our Lord. You are the All-Glorious with irresistible might, the All-Wise. (al-Mumtahina 60:5)

Abraham, peace be upon him, opened up to God thus, expressed his trust in Him, and sought refuge in His protection. This is the way those with sincere belief monitor themselves; this is how they are in their own eyes, and show their deep relationship with God within.

Prophet Jacob (peace be upon him)

The Qur'an devotes a wide section to Jacob (Yaqub), peace be upon him, as another monumental person of "facing the self." He had a deep love for his mission; he went the extra mile with painstaking endeavors to give his position its due, and having internalized his responsibility, he lived with a desire to extinguish many sparks of unbelief and corruption popping up on all sides. He preached to many obstinate ones the discipline of relations with God that he inherited from his forerunners.

While fulfilling these heavy responsibilities with the punctiliousness of a Prophet, Jacob (pbuh) was subjected to a different trial by means of his children. His sons' inability to stomach Joseph (pbuh) would upset this sensitive soul. With his compassion as a father, his sensibility as a Prophet, and his relations with the realms beyond, he saw his son Joseph as a person to bear the trust from Abraham and Isaac, and thus showed an extra care for him. However, since other sons were not aware of these inward considerations of his—probably they had not reached that level of spiritual and moral maturity—they continually ate their hearts out with plans to get rid of Joseph. In the end, they did what they had planned and took him away from their father.

That wicked incident fell on Jacob (pbuh) like a nightmare; that innocent and protected soul felt as if struck by a thunderbolt as he grieved Joseph's disappearance and the cruelty and lies of his sons. His senses were very sharp; none of the things asserted as pretext and consolation seemed convincing to him. He did not fall to hopelessness; he maintained his expectations alive and alert, but the incident was an upsetting one. At such a time when material causes were lost from sight and his spirit was trapped with dismay, "the mystery of God's absolute Oneness (*ahadiyya*) manifested within the light of Divine Unity (*tawhid*)";[9] thus, he turned to God's door – his eternal sanctuary – with an *extraordinary* effort, which was in fact his *ordinary* state of being, for his face, eyes, ears, and heart were always attentive to that door.

Jacob, peace be upon him, opened up to Him with the profundity of having annihilated himself in the Divine (*fana fillah*), wailed and moaned, and said: "*I complain of my anguish and sorrow only to God, and I know from God what you do not know*" (Yusuf 12:86). In a serious mood of reliance on and submission to God, he took a consoling breath with a "beautiful patience" (Yusuf 12:83), committed his affairs to God, and let himself wait for a dawn of Divine mercy.

His inward self-criticism as well as Joseph's conduct of rectitude and Prophetic intelligence served as a call for Divine providence. The sequence of events that started with a dream was concluded with a relieving reunion after so many surprise happenings—like Joseph's being saved from the well safe and sound, being exonerated from the plot of women, turning the prison into a place of edification, providing guidance to many people who had gone astray and helping them with inspirations of his heart in the name of God, being promoted as a minister thanks to the gift of interpreting dreams and happenings, and doing extra favors to his brothers who had mistreated him.

In the words of M. Lütfi Efendi,

> *The garden of the nightingale singing for the Beloved appeared,*
> *The season for the tulips in the clime of the Friend appeared.*
> *That day the scent of Joseph reached Jacob,*
> *And to everyone, how the river of life runs became evident.*

And thus, that succession of bitter and grievous days came to an end, as Jacob (pbuh) was already sure of it. From the very beginning, he had come to grips with his inner world, opened up to God and wailed;

9   This is in reference to Bediüzzaman Said Nursi's description of Prophet Jonah's (Yunus) being delivered from darkness upon darkness as a clear sign of God's unique and absolute Oneness, for He is the only one with full authority over the whale, the sea, the night, and all other causes.

now it was time for reaping the harvest of what he had gone through. In accordance with the principle, "gains will be proportionate to the pains taken,"[10] he remained steadfast in the face of successive troubles and curbed his suffering within, to not let his woe influence other feelings. And then he lived with gratitude to God effected by worldly and otherworldly happiness.

May the All-Just Lord let the sufferers and oppressed ones in our time reach these horizons also! Amen!

Prophet Joseph (peace be upon him)

We partially referred to Joseph (Yusuf), peace be upon him, in the shade of his father. His story was a very special one. He was a perfected person and an exemplary figure with his reliance on and submission to God, not wavering despite what befell him. His steadfastness, his upright stance in the face of situations to provoke carnal desires, his innocence, and his loyalty to God turned prison into a place of edification.

He was subjected to pressures and assaults in every phase of his life. He welcomed what fate decreed for him with contentment, he turned each of them into an advantage and a means of goodness. He was a locus of manifestations of providence and a notable in the eyes of high assembly of angels (*al-mala al-a'la*) (Saffaat 37:8). For him, the bottom of the well became an observatory for "the mystery of God's absolute Oneness manifested within the light of Divine Unity."

His being sold like a slave—may our souls be sacrificed for that slave—enabled him to observe the lifestyles of the upper elite; his entrance to the dungeon served as a means for his purity and profundity to be seen and known, and each point that seemed evil served as a step for ascending to his future mission. In his childhood and adolescence, he always lived under Divine guardianship. In his later life, he took refuge in the stronghold of faith and ascended to the exalted position of being the favorite one of those on earth and in the heavens.

When they could not manage to seduce him, he was threatened with prison. He said, *"My Lord! Prison is dearer to me than what they bid me to. If You do not avert their guile from me, I might incline towards them*

and become one of the ignorant (those who succumb to such temptations)"
(Yusuf 12:33).

He went to the dungeon with consent. He was young, charming,
and in full health for desires of the flesh, but his immaculate feeling of
decency, perfect God-consciousness, and his feeling of and yearning for
seeing God and gaining His good pleasure were so deep as to make him
oblivious of himself.

Then a time came when he interpreted the king's dream correctly
thanks to his knowledge of the inner meaning of happenings inspired by
God, while others dismissed it as "jumbled images." Following this, he
became a minister of the king.

When the women admitted their guilt, their statements of ex-
oneration did not change him at all. With serious self-effacement and
modesty he said, *"Yet I do not claim myself free of error, for assuredly the
human carnal soul always commands evil, except that my Lord has mercy
(which saves us from committing evil acts). Surely my Lord is All-Forgiv-
ing, All-Compassionate"* (Yusuf 12:53). With a virtuous attitude special to
the Prophets, he walked to his happy future with a becoming magnanimity. The attitude his brothers adopted before this monument of decency,
innocence, and Prophetic intelligence is a subject that merits separate
consideration.

This sequence of events was foretold in a dream, and its finale was a
joyful celebration when the family finally reunited. While everybody was
elated by this profound joy, Prophet Joseph (pbuh) turned to his eternal
sanctuary in a way perfected persons have always done:

> My Lord, You have indeed granted me an important part of the rule
> and knowledge of the inner meaning of happenings; O my Lord,
> Originator of the heavens and the earth with a dizzying harmony! You
> are my Owner and Guardian in this world and in the Hereafter. Take
> my soul to You as a Muslim, and join me with the righteous (Yusuf
> 12:101).

As Joseph was crying out this supplication, he was emphasizing the
fact that those tempted by the world and worldliness are in a delusion,
which, to me, is one of the heartstrings of the matter. After having completed his mission, Joseph (pbuh) pushed aside the world in a way which

can be described best with the words of the poet Fuzuli: *"How pleasant to my soul if the Beloved asked for it / What worth is my soul anyway that I should not sacrifice it for my Beloved?"* Or in other words: *When the Beloved asks for my soul, how is it possible not to give it / How can we complain; my soul is neither yours nor mine.*

Joseph (pbuh) was indeed a hero of the heart and spirit, who always led a life oriented to his eternal sanctuary; a towering figure of faith we should envy.

Prophet Shu'ayb (peace be upon him)

Prophet Shu'ayb[11] spent his life shuttling between Midian (Madyan) and Aykah. He stood upright with an inner immensity despite his people's corruption, denial, and unruliness. According to works of Qur'anic exegesis, Shu'ayb (pbuh) is the righteous person who sheltered Moses (Musa), peace be upon them, and let him marry his daughter. With his Prophetic insight, he discovered Moses to be an important paragon of Divine mission and kept him near himself for years like his own child.

God Almighty entrusted a future Messenger (Moses) to another Messenger (Shu'ayb) who gladly welcomed this trust of God and opened his bosom to it. Like all Prophets, Shu'ayb (pbuh) prioritized calling people to faith in God. Besides this important mission, he struggled against social and economic speculations; in the blessed light of Divine revelation, he tried to establish social justice in society.

Like the rebellious ones at the time of Prophet Noah, degenerates at the time of Prophet Hud, and the transgressors at the time of Prophet Salih, Prophet Shu'ayb's people also opposed him with denial, obstinacy, and derision. Moreover, they forced that exalted Messenger to accept their false belief. He responded to these with the equanimity and valor of a Messenger, and, like other Messengers did, he made clear as a man of God that he was not after any worldly wealth: he never asked of people for rewards or wages in return for this mission.[12] Sadly, they did not believe and took him lightly; so he warned them of the Divine retribution, which

---

11   Prophet Shu'ayb (pbuh) is traditionally identified with the Biblical Jethro, Prophet Moses' father-in-law.

12   Yunus 10:72; Hud 11:29, 51; ash-Shuara 26:109, 127, 145, 164, 180; Saba 34:47.

was an unchanging Divine law. While Prophet Shu'ayb called them to God and eternal bliss, obstinate masses kept forcing him to accept their crooked and false belief with different pressures, as it happened in the past and present. He had no other choice but to leave them to the Divine retribution decreed for them. The answer of the Messenger was clear:

> *Should we return to your way after God has saved us from it, then most certainly we would be fabricating lies in attribution to God. It is not for us to turn back to it, unless God, our Lord, should so will. Our Lord embraces all things within His Knowledge. In God do we put our trust. Our Lord! Judge between us and our people, making the truth manifest, for You are the Best in judging to make the truth manifest.* (al-A'raf 7:89)

He implored and wailed, incurring the protective care of the Divine, and eventually one day, and—as is always the case—tyrants received their just deserts: they were destroyed by a shocking catastrophe. As for those who shared the honor of siding with the Truth, by feeling both the joy of deliverance and a pity deep inside for those destroyed, they kept walking on their righteous path to God.

The Divine tradition has never changed from past to present. Wails of the oppressed and mistreated have always existed along with growls of oppressors and tyrants. And when one day their lamentation amounts to incurring the protective care of the Divine, despotic ones fall into their own trap, whereas the righteous ones with clear consciences feel sorry for them having already forgotten what they suffered from them.

Prophet Moses (peace be upon him)

What a story is the life of Prophet Moses (Musa)—*Kalimullah*, the one honored with Divine speech.

When he was left to his fate in the river, he was still in the cradle. He then was looked after until a certain age by his archenemies. He had to leave his homeland, Egypt, after an unfortunate incident. In his new place, he was homesick, but he had to fulfill an agreement he made with his host, which became his spiritual journeying. His retreats were not just forty days or weeks, but years – his life was filled with suffering just as his predecessors did. As we learn from one hadith, the Prophets were the most severely tested among all people.[13] Accordingly, he did suffer throughout his life, but he would never whine about the troubles he went through.

His opening up to God, fully turning to Him, and coming to grips with himself happened with the unintended death of a Copt he had knocked down with a punch. God forgave him after he felt remorse and pleaded, *"My Lord! Indeed, I have wronged myself, so forgive me. My Lord! Forasmuch as You have blessed me with favors, I will never be a supporter of the guilty"* (al-Qasas 28:16-17).

Such was the state and condition of those great personages; they saw as major sins things we dismiss as trivial or do not see at all, and they rushed to seek forgiveness. And God was always directing them to the horizons of remaining clear and pure.

Moses (pbuh) had a certain mission: preaching to the tyrant of his time about God and leading the Children of Israel to a safe land. But, in the time of Moses, Pharaohs held the power in Egypt, and they would either kill or imprison everyone opposing them—just like the pharaohs of our time do. It was difficult to carry out the Divine orders received in Mount Sinai. However, when the command was Divine, it was not possible to say no. He had to fulfill his Prophetic mission to invite people to God and also to save the Children of Israel from the despotism and cruelty of those oppressors worse than the devil. Though his blessed soul was newly crowned with heavenly revelation, upon the Divine command he set to deal with the issue without hesitation by taking his brother Prophet Aaron in his company. He boldly faced different challenges by putting his trust in the Creator's grace and guardianship.

The problems he endured were not limited to the ones caused by obdurate rulers: there were those who said they would not accept faith if Moses (pbuh) did not show God to them openly. There were those who took the opportunity of his temporary absence and – urged by Satan – to worship the statue of a calf. There were also faithless ones on his side who complained, *"We suffered hurt before you came to us, and since you came to us!"* (al-A'raf 7:129).

And when troubles were overcome and they reached a land of deliverance, there were some mindless ones who said, "O Moses, make for us

13   Thirmidhi, *Zuhd*, 57, Ibn Maja, *Fitan*, 23, Darimi, *Riqaq*, 67.

a god, as they have gods..." (al-A'raf 7:138). There were some ill-mannered ones who resisted entering a certain place where they were supposed to fight a war. They were so insolent to say, *"Go forth, then, you and your Lord, and fight, both of you. We will be sitting just here!"* (al-Ma'idah 5:24).

Against all odds, Moses (pbuh) took his elder brother Aaron with him and never ceased to fulfill God's commands until the day he passed away in the desert of the Tih. Though there were times when he left the impertinent ones before him—including the Copts—to Divine retribution, he never gave up on his mission. He always undertook it with a serious feeling of reliance on and submission to God Almighty.

I don't know whether these words mean anything to the guides of our time and their followers who stagger on their way. It is my hope that there will be new generations to spread the truths of the Qur'an who will walk in the footsteps of these exemplary figures, satisfy the hunger and thirst of all humanity, and will make that awaited revival come true. Why not as long as God wills it?

Prophet Jonah (peace be upon him)

One of the brilliant figures of history who was able to "read" himself was Jonah (Yunus), peace be upon him, also known as "Dhu'n Nun." His eyes were set to seeking the good pleasure of God with a trembling heart filled with the awe and grandeur of the Divine.

He was sent to a city called Nineveh to call people to God. But the people of this land failed to appreciate his mission. Despite all his efforts, they persisted in their disbelief, and eventually he started perceiving signals of a Divine chastisement upon them. This had been the fate of all such people who opposed their Prophet and insisted on unbelief; deniers were either drowned in waters, or sunk to the ground, or were destroyed with stones from the heavens. That exalted Messenger saw the signs of such a fate to befall his people, and he adopted a conduct similar to his forerunners: he left this land. However, given the conditions that are binding those closest to God, was it the right thing to do at that point to leave his post without a direct Divine command; this is a very fine point to consider!

Jonah (pbuh) embarked on a ship, and what followed is commonly known. Thrown into the sea and swallowed by a whale, this great Messenger profoundly felt his helplessness with a full conviction that apparent causes had no power whatsoever. With a Prophetic consciousness and commitment to God, he was inspired with "the mystery of God's absolute Oneness within the light of Divine Unity" – he turned to his eternal sanctuary, to the door of the Unique One of Absolute Unity. He came to grips with himself, and moaned and implored God as follows:

> *There is no deity but you, All-Glorified You are. Surely, I have been one of the wrongdoers.* (al-Anbiya 21:87)

A quick response was given to his cry, and he found himself in the shade of a gourd plant. He was restored to life after his profound opening up and humble entreaty to God. He turned to the location he was supposed to be, and became a means of a new revival for thousands of people. As those with wisdom do, he knew that God Almighty would never let down and abundantly reward those who turned to Him and implored with awareness of their natural state of being in need of Him.

If only the wronged and oppressed of today, when apparent causes seem so adverse, would turn to their eternal sanctuary with such a mood and petition God in tears. Maybe one day they will; let us hope that it will not be too late by then.

Prophet Job (peace be upon him)

Job (Ayyub), peace be upon him, was a distinguished figure with his reverence for God, his refined soul, his spirit of submission to God, and his life on the horizons of *tafwiz* (committing affairs to God). As a Prophet he was no different from the other "chosen and the righteous" ones (Saad 38:47) in terms of his view of the world, considerations of the Afterlife, and his scrupulous care about living up to his special Prophetic virtues.

It is mentioned in some works, whose sources are open to debate, that he was granted abundant wealth as a result of his lawful gains. This should of course be considered in line with his Prophetic character: as all of those closest to God do, he too totally shut the doors of his fine heart against worldly expectations and in accordance with the truth, "*Truly, God provides to whomever He wills without reckoning*" (Al Imran 3:37). Job's (pbuh) entire wealth was at the disposal of his altruism; his priority was to breathe life to others. This being the case, even if he had owned much greater wealth than Korah, it would still be just fine. Given that the heart is not contaminated and thus would not lose its reality of being a mirror to the Divine, what is earned as extra Divine bestowals are categorized as worldly blessings and asking for such blessings is not wrong. If he truly owned such wealth and had many children as in the narrations about him, what falls to us is to say, "Let it be so."

Here is a summary of his case: When all of his wealth was unexpectedly taken away, he stood firm with dignity: "God had given them, and now He has taken them away." At another time, when his children and kindred were also taken away from him, the same golden words came out of the lips of that Prophet whose heart was beating with the same spirit of entrusting affairs to God. After some time, he was inflicted by a number of diseases; he remained steadfast and took refuge in the fortress of becoming, beautiful patience (*sabrun jamil*). However, when those diseases finally amounted to such a degree that, in the description of Bediüzzaman, he feared his heart and tongue could no longer fulfill their duties to worship his Lord.[14] Only after this point, this blessed Prophet, who screened his worry even from other feelings in his heart, petitioned God with a mannerly supplication—without being over-demanding and without showing insolent insistence: "*O my Lord! Truly, affliction has visited me; and You are the Most Merciful of the merciful*" (al-Anbiya 21:83). Thus, God Almighty decreed: "*We answered his prayer and removed all the afflictions from which he suffered; and restored to him his household and the like thereof along with them as a mercy from Us and as a reminder to those devoted to Our worship*" (al-Anbiya 21:84). God took back what He had given once and subjected that hero of patience to a trial this way. Later on, in return for his patience and loyalty, God rewarded him with much more than He had taken away and let him rejoice.

In another chapter of the Qur'an, we find him ascribing the disease to Satan. The Divine revelation conveys the issue as follows:

> *And remember Our servant, Job, when he called out to his Lord: "Surely Satan has caused me to be afflicted with distress and great suffering."* (Saad 38:41)

This prayer was both a confession of the exalted Prophet's vulner-

14   See: Nursi, *The Gleams*, Second Gleam.

ability against Satan on one hand—as much as it applies to those closest to God—and an effort to glorify God by attributing what befell to him to Satan instead.

***

In this article, we tried to talk about those "chosen, righteous" ones (Saad 38:47) in what can amount to nothing more than a drop from the ocean in comparison to their mighty status: they had a unique relationship with God; they led their lives under an exceptional self-supervision, and they were scrupulous about manners and attitudes they deemed unbecoming for them (whose actual nature is unknown to us as we know that sins did not contaminate even their dreams). God knows the truth of the issue, but probably even angels in heavens envied such profundity and beheld them in admiration. How we wish we could share the atom of such an approach. Unfortunately, most of us are not even aware of our bearing the filth of sins—particularly those in the lead!

FACING THE SELF – THE FIRST CIRCLE

The noble Messenger, Muhammad, peace and blessings be upon him, was like a sun: his advent lit up all eras and outshined all other stars. He was a brilliant moon whose light was from the Sun of all suns. With his advent in the physical world, an effulgent circle was formed around him and his blessed light. Those who formed this circle were the first fortunate ones who welcomed his reviving breaths from the pulpit of Prophethood. God's Messenger called these blessed ones who followed him so punctiliously and who were imbued with his resplendent hue as "my stars." Following these stars, he reminded, is a means of deliverance for those who embrace his teachings.

None of the things that he stated or thought remained up in the air; the heavenly light that came from the beyond and reflected in that pristine mirror turned into a blessed circle of light around him. He constantly conveyed that light of lights to this blessed constellation, and those bright souls internalizing that radiant moon clustered like a halo around him, and each became a pristine mirror. With a slight editing to the original, this couplet of the poet Nabi describes their situation so beautifully:

In the seat of Prophethood he is in the center of the circle of light
The full moon that expounds to stars the meaning of the "verse of the light."

Those apt souls, each of whom became a bright mirror of that full moon in a very short time, formed a halo around that illustrious guide

87

and attained an immense and dazzling radiance whose essential source was from the beyond and even further. They were constantly hovering like moths around that source of light as they reflected the heavenly qualities of their role model. It was thanks to this exceptional privilege, along with their own excellence and profundity, that they presented an astonishing example to the world through their modest, self-effacing, unpretentious, and constantly self-critical stance. It would not be an exaggeration to say that the four Rightly Guided Caliphs from among this circle were incomparably eminent and made the dwellers of the heavens envy them. Along with their status in heart and spirit, they always subjected themselves to severe criticism and saw themselves as if they were a—God forbid—sinful person.

Abu Bakr (may God be pleased with him)

Abu Bakr, may God be pleased with him, was one of the most notable ones of this circle. He beheld the blessed lights and mysteries of the beyond – and perhaps even further beyond – in the mirror of the noble Messenger, the beloved of his heart and our hearts, who was his fresh spring and source of spiritual nourishment.

Abu Bakr was the Faithful One (al-Siddiq) and had the honor of being praised by the beloved Prophet. Yet, when he opened up to God in self-criticism, he supplicated as follows:

> "My God, I surely did much wrongdoing to my own soul; there is no one else to forgive my sins but You. Please forgive me, grant me a pardon, and have mercy on me. Surely You are the sole One Who forgives sins much, Who grants particular mercy."

O the dearly beloved, even during the Age of Ignorance you did not have any sins, not even in your dream; if we are to take these wails and moans as an outcome of being one of the closest of the close to God, then I say, may God forgive us for the sake of your prayers, and curb my sinful tongue with a lock. If your words are a statement in the sense of giving a guideline to future generations, then I woe for our own condition.

Abu Bakr, may God be pleased with him, never went astray in his blessed life and always turned to God with dedication. How come does this eminent personality mention "sins" about himself and is asking forgiveness? He was above all the first and foremost of the earliest ones who took their place in that circle of light. When Prophet Muhammad, that Glorious Nightingale and mirror of the Divine, was seeking a person to welcome the revelation from beyond this world, Abu Bakr was the foremost to come with a vigilant heart.

He was such a faithful one who lived by deepening this acceptance until the end of his life. In order to protect the Prophet, he acted like a guardian angel for the first thirteen years of Islam in Mecca, in a way to be comparable to the "believer from the Pharaoh's family" (at the time of Prophet Moses) (al-Mumin 40:28-30). He said yes to the most dangerous expedition with the beloved Prophet when death was at their doorstep— and he did so without the slightest hesitation. During their stopover in the majestical cave of Thawr, he was deeply concerned for the protection of his beloved.

When they were saved from all troubles and arrived at their illustrious Medina, he continued his heroism as enviable as would be by the angels. Yet, he would push all these merits into oblivion and was always an ordinary person when he opened up to God. He adopted the words of his blessed guide, God's Messenger (pbuh)—may our souls be sacrificed for that guide! In his supplications, Abu Bakr beseeched so deeply that angels would be absorbed in contemplation and admiration. Here are a few drops from his words:

> "Please vouchsafe with blessings Your poor servant, whose provisions are so little, who came to Your door as a loser, O the All-Majestic One! His sins are so gross; please forgive his sins. He is a poor and a sinful, lowly slave. From him are transgression, forgetfulness, and successive errs; he is expecting from You bountiful favors and grace..."

> "What is to become of me, while I have no good deed, my misdeeds are so much in excess, and my merits and devotions are so little. Please order the fires to become cool, O Lord! Just as you did before, for the sake of the Khalil (Prophet Abraham)!"

What a vigorous and wholehearted self-criticism and turning to God; what a profound beseeching and immense self-supervision this is!

He was the paragon of faithfulness; yet, he opened up to God in the manner of an ordinary person. As a matter of fact, he was blessed with many successes which were not conferred even to many Prophets, including his leadership when countless armed conflicts and rebellions were suppressed. Above all, he was directly praised by the Prophet. But none of these sufficed to moderate his severe self-criticism that was permeated with a sharp awareness of being seen by God (the state of *ihsan*).

He was an outstanding statesman, an exemplar of fairness and justice, and a high character who never wavered or slipped. Each episode of his life was like a separate legend of heroism.[1] His spirit was as pure as the angels and was never beguiled by these merits; he always trembled with righteous concerns behind his guide. He kept interrogating himself. While doing so, he was virtually oblivious to his accomplishments, which would normally take centuries for other people to achieve.

If only these considerations could mean something to the selfish degenerates of our time who make a mountain out of a molehill! Sadly, those reckless ones never saw these nor did they make any effort to see and think about them; worldliness has made them blind and deaf. Their life is passing in the narrow corridors of corporeality. They are unaware of the meaning of having a faithful life oriented to the spirit and the heart. Waking people up requires an extra grace from God. We always maintain our hopes in God's immense mercy, but I do not think these degenerates will come to their senses. As I leave such an awakening to an extra grace from Divine Providence, let us continue with another monumental personage.

Umar ibn al-Khattab (may God be pleased with him)

Umar ibn al-Khattab was the sun of justice. This illustrious personage on the path of the Prophets was exceptionally scrupulous at keeping up the conduct of those closest to God. He was on earth, but lived an immensely enviable life of heart and spirit on a par with heavenly beings. He was honored by constant appreciations of the Prophet (pbuh), and he broke manifold records of accomplishment by realizing within ten years what so many great states, including the Ottomans, could only realize in a century.

1   See *Abkariyyat* by Mahmud Akkad.

In spite of these incredible credentials, Umar took his illustrious place in the circle around the Last Prophet with modesty, humbleness, and a manner of being ordinary; he was a matchless and unreachable person whose status on earth was – as the Prophet described him – that of the archangel Michael in the heavens.[2]

Umar inherited a heavenly heritage whose sound foundations had been laid by the perfect guide, Muhammad (pbuh), and the first caliph, Abu Bakr. He presented an outstanding performance on benefiting from this heritage and carrying it forward to a stupendous level. With strength and power from God, and spiritual support from the blessed guide, Muhammad (pbuh), Umar made believers elated and left hypocrites disappointed.

Until the end of his blessed life, he showed a performance like Dhu'l-Qarnayn[3] with successive victories, and as he was giving his last in this transient realm he chose a most appropriate successor, Uthman ibn Affan.

With a consideration of being a neighbor in the grave to his guide [the Prophet, pbuh], whose company he would not exchange for the entire world, he wished to be buried in the blessed chamber of the Prophet's mosque, and so was his wish granted. He wholeheartedly believed in the Messenger of God and loved him in the ultimate degree, as it would be expected from such a noble soul who was way above normal human standards.

Umar lived as the "second vizier" (in reference to the Prophetic hadith mentioned above), a hero of willpower, and a paragon of self-annihilation (*fana fillah*) and permanence (*baqa billah*) with God. He was neither dizzied by routing superpowers nor conquering lands, nor being applauded for his righteousness and justice. He was even disturbed by being called "the leader of believers" by faithful persons who admired his fairness and rectitude, and always warned those around him in this

2   This is in reference to a hadith in which Prophet Muhammad, peace be upon him, stated that he had two viziers in the world and two in the heavens; those in the world were Abu Bakr and Umar, and those in heavens were Gabriel and Michael (Al-Hakim, *al-Mustadrak*, 2/290).

3   Dhu'l-Qarnayn is a heroic figure mentioned in the Qur'an (al-Kahf 18:83–101) as one who travels to east and west and sets up a barrier between a certain people and Gog and Magog.

matter. He always regarded himself as an ordinary person among others even while he was at the highest possible position. He neither had any bodyguards nor any security detail. He said "I put my trust in the hands of God"[4] and was always among the people on his own—if only all of this meant something to the pharaohs and tyrants of our age! However, my conscience does not believe presumptuous fools with dead hearts and poisoned thoughts will ever understand anything from these examples. Let us return to our actual subject by emphasizing that any advice and examples will be in vain for the unfortunate ones who try to appear that they are something although they are nothing, and who have no interest in being ordinary people.

The Prophet gave the glad tidings that Umar would realize fabulous things. Once, he saw a dream in which Umar was vigorously drawing water from a well and all the people there drank their fill.[5] This dream was only one of many future achievements of Umar as they appeared to the Messenger of God from the lacework of fate in the realm of meanings and ideal forms. In spite of his many wonderful deeds, outstanding abilities, character, and activities that would make angels salute him, he saw himself as nobody. *"Bring yourself to account, before you are brought to account"*[6] was the guiding principle of his blessed life.

His heart-rending petitions were with the diamond words from the diamond-like prayers of the Prophet and his predecessor, Abu Bakr. His heart-rendering entreaties were like pearl drop annotations to these

---

4   *"Tawakkaltu 'alallah"* (I put my trust in the hands of God) is a part of a prayer the
     Prophet teaches Muslims to say before leaving home for protection and guidance.
     "Tawakkul" is to do one's best and to leave the outcome to God (*Riyad as-Salihin*,
     83).

5   The Prophet said, "I saw (in a dream) the people assembled in a gathering, and
     then Abu Bakr got up and drew one or two buckets of water (from a well) but there
     was weakness in his drawing. May Allah forgive him. Then Umar took the bucket,
     and in his hands it turned into a very large bucket. I had never seen anyone who
     could draw the water as strongly as Umar did. (He drew water) until all the people
     drank their fill and watered their camels that knelt down there" (Bukhari, *Book 61*,
     Hadith 138).

6   Tirmidhi, *Qiyama*, 25; Ibnu'l-Mubarak, *Zuhd*, 1:103; Ibn Abi Shayba, *al-Musan-
     naf*, 7/96.

prayers in the form of wails and moans. He constantly recited what the Prophet, the matchless guide, had stated in self-criticism in accordance with his horizons of the closest of the close to God. He used those jewel-like angelic words at his opening up to and imploring God. Whatever the Prophet said and whichever arguments he used while opening up to God, they were working up and down in Umar's heart, just as was the case for the Prophet and Abu Bakr.

What a purity, what a soundness in proximity to God! While struggling with so many challenges, Umar always proceeded on the horizons of the Prophets, and he always spent an important part of his time murmuring the name of God. He was utilizing his life—night and day, and day and week—by constantly opening up to God and bringing himself to account for sins that he did not commit, as is the case with those closest to God. His words could be paraphrased with the following hymn:

> *My sins are beyond limits, have mercy on me, O God;*
> *My tears are flowing blood, have mercy on me, O God!*

Throughout his life, there was not a single moment without self-interrogation. Here are a few drops from those episodes of coming to grips with himself and self-supervision:

"My God, protect me to live upon Islam while standing, sitting, and sleeping in bed! My God, bless me with the goodness in Your possession and protect this poor one from evils! My God, enable this slave of Yours to consider the Manifest Book at heart with the most serious deliberation and contemplation! Forgive me and accept my repentance! My heart is hard and nobody is aware of that hardness." [*O my sultan, if you call realizing justice as hardness of the heart, this is something special to your high horizons and we bow to salute this refined understanding of yours. F.G.*]

"Please treat me leniently with Your magnanimity concerning my deeds I have done for the world beyond! My God! I am one of Your miserly servants." [*O my dear one, who did not own any wealth in this world, tell me O the light of my eye, if even you call yourself miserly, then who else deserves to be called generous! F.G.*]

"Please enable me to always behave sincerely without falling to waste-fulness and without straying to show off in affectation. Render me among Your servants who solely dream of Your good pleasure and the Hereafter in my every condition and behavior! My God! I have been very heedless and forgetful." [*O Umar, my shining light, these are only an expression of your perfection! God, please seal the mouths of those who badmouth him by taking his self-critical words as real! F.G.*]

"O God, let Your Umar be one of Your servants who always dream of You, of the reality of death, and what lies beyond! My God, I am rather weak in terms of worship." [*O my brilliant master, were you not the one who cried at prostration and made others in the mosque cry with you? F. G.*]

"Please grant me purity of intention and vigor at my worship!"

These humble petitions of repentance, these inner cries and self-criticisms belong to the illustrious Umar; Umar who enkindled in hearts love for God and His Messenger across wide territories. My words here fall short to present him as he deserves. Umar pushes the entirety of his merits into oblivion and sincerely petitions God, in a way to astonish angels, with the manner of an ordinary man. These were the breaths of the closest of those closest to God, Umar, the paragon of justice, who showed the way to revival for those to follow.

On seeing those of pure character, people with vigilant consciences sigh with appreciation and say, "If only a hundredth of this refinement and profundity were to be found in the degenerates of today who wor-ship their selves and money!"

Before I wrap up, I feel like making the following address to you Oh, Umar: You and your predecessor, like that absolute guide you both followed, always led such a profound life envied by the angels. You virtu-ally became an exemplary compass for tired wayfarers like us who stag-ger their way on. Most people have not understood the actual meaning, the true color, and pattern of leading a life like yours! If we and certain degenerates dizzy with worldliness and blurred vision could, then our world could have become something like a utopia. What a pity: by know-ingly preferring worldliness over the realms beyond and even further beyond, these degenerates have caused successive disappointments for themselves and others. The entire world is seeing followers of Islam as terrorists because of them. And Muslims, we, have had to pay a high price for this.

Oh, Umar, you stand so inaccessibly mighty. If I have taken you lower than your immense horizons with my broken statements in this article, give it to my misery and forgive this humble servant, please! I have always told your story so many times and will continue to do so. It is impossible for me not to continue, because with your blessed lives you all became a source of wise inspirations cherished in our hearts thanks to the guidance of the Last Prophet, who pointed out: *"Upon you is my tradition and the tradition of the Rightly Guided Caliphs."*[7]

Uthman ibn Affan (may God be pleased with him)

The next in the circle is Uthman, the one with the pure light of the All-Merciful reflecting on his face. He was called "the Possessor of Two Lights" (Dhun Nurayn), because he became the Prophet's son-in-law twice.[8] Here are a few drops of his entreaties, resembling those of a Prophet in terms of their inner profundity. The shortcomings at reflecting their true level in this article are purely my own.

In Uthman's inner world, one could hear his laments for almost twenty-five years after the passing of the Prophet, which resonated like the touching sound of a reed flute, until his own demise. These laments were coming from his heart and spirit, yet they were in fact sighs and petitions of the Prophet (pbuh), each a reviving elixir to whoever recites them. Uthman was so noble that he probably thought adding words from himself would contaminate the words of the Prophet that were like the water of life from heaven. With such considerations and fidelity, he preferred to offer his petitions to God Almighty with the same compositions of the Prophet.

His atlas of feelings and thoughts were the same with his predecessors. His eyes were fixed on the eyes of the Prophet, and he was all

---

7   Tirmidhi, *'Ilm*, 16; Abu Dawud, *Sunnah*, 5; Ibn Maja, *Muqaddima*, 6.

8   After Ruqayya died, the Prophet married Uthman with another of his daughters, Umm Kulthum.

ears for what he said. As a result of his outstanding modesty and beauty of character, Uthman's imploring, petition, and sighs always took place within the frame of what the former had said and done. In his own manners, he took as basis all that he learned from the Messenger of God, who, Uthman thought in complete submission, already said all that was necessary which needed to be taken as habitual recitations. He constantly lived with the feeling of respect for his predecessors and regarded behaving otherwise as digression from the proper course. He did not show his inner suffering; he did not appear as someone who held himself accountable all the time. Yet, he did, and he did so privately, like *khalwatis* (who observe their worship in retreat). He and his predecessors were in the footsteps of the Pride of Humanity (pbuh) so scrupulously: like a jewel master with the magnifier of their insight ensuring that the lyrics and composition were the same, and with the same touching tunes.

The Messenger of God (pbuh) petitioned with words that were the crown of all; the lyrics and tunes of his successors were the same with the sole difference being their voice. They were like illustrious mirrors that reflected everything in its original form in the circle of that radiant moon. They turned to God and came to grips with their own soul with the same arguments, pattern, and rhythm voiced by their Glorious Guide (pbuh). They shook with concern not to be off course from the Prophet's words and manners of imploring God, which made them very scrupulous at using his language in every state of theirs.

Uthman, the Possessor of Two Lights, was blessed with a refinement of spirit, immense mannerliness and bashfulness, as well as with his kinship with the noble Prophet. He breathed with the blessed Messenger's words, manners, and imploring spirit. Besides all of these, he would touch the doorknob of Divine mercy with the spirit found in the following hymn[9]:

> *Everything is from You, You are the truly rich*
> *My Lord, I have turned my face to You!*
> *You are the All-Preceding, You are the Everlasting*
> *My Lord, I have turned my face to You!*

9   This hymn is written by Fethullah Gülen.

Uthman took the Qur'an as the basis of his sighs and a means of supplication, and he would seek refuge in God by concluding with a selection of verses including *al-Mu'awwidhatayn,* the two short chapters of refuge (Falaq and Nas). Until the moment some ill-fated ones martyred him, he would continue this special selection of recitations. The drops of blood upon the paper of the Qur'an are the loyal witnesses of his heartfelt connection with the Divine Speech. He had always opened and closed his eyes with the Qur'an – and as he gave his last, the Divine Word closed his eyes for the last time to the world.

Today, there are ill-fated ones who hold the Qur'an in their hands and tongues but with worldly considerations in their heart. May God Almighty let them thoroughly feel the spirit of the Qur'an and save them from paying lip service to it, and may He guide them to a proper life oriented to the horizons of the heart and spirit.

Ali ibn Abu Talib (may God be pleased with him)

Habibullah (the beloved one of God) was Prophet Muhammad Mustafa, peace be upon him, and Waliyullah (chief saint of God) was Ali al-Murtaza (the one who attained the pleasure of God). From the moment he opened his eyes to life, Ali grew up as a paragon of purity, and he would later come to be known as a valiant warrior (Haidar-i Karrar), conqueror of Khaybar, and son-in-law to the Prophet. He did not let anything taint his name. His life constantly reflected how eligible he was for the merit of being the prince of saints. He stood up to the most challenging troubles, putting his life at stake for the Messenger of God (pbuh).

Like his predecessors, Ali, too, always said what the Guide of the world (pbuh) said about "facing the self" and opening up to God; he wailed like the Messenger (pbuh) and walked in his footsteps. However, when one day Ali saw himself surrounded in a spiral of different troubles, he let himself to a profound entreaty, petitioning, and opening up to God in pain. He did so because he was a responsible believer and as an outcome of circumstances, but he never compromised from the essential disciplines of turning to God. He set about opening up to God in different supplications, both in terms of being saved from the troubles he was facing and holding himself to account. The suffering accumulated in his heart turned into petitions in his tongue in different hues and patterns in response to the turbulent character of his era when many heart-rending calamities occurred one after the other. This strange and new situation led him to use a new language: with his rich power of expression, he left behind as a heritage a new style of entreating and petitioning God for those to follow him later on. His blessed life always passed with a stream of woes and moans of supplication to God. He constantly turned to Divine court with the sincerest feelings and was presenting his condition to his most Compassionate Lord as follows:

> "My God! You are the sole Sovereign; no other deities exist, and You are my All-Generous Lord. I am a servant at Your door. I committed so many evils." [*O Ali, I can only say, "Never" about what you are saying here. F. G.*]

> "I have wronged my soul; here I am in Your presence and I confess my sins." [*if only I knew what you call sin! F. G.*]

> "O the Much Forgiving, the All-Responsive, the Wise, Compassionate Lord! Forgive my sins please! No one else but You can forgive sins. I seek refuge in You against all harms that can possibly befall me, against losing everything, falling to disgrace, grievous and worrisome situations, and against remaining helpless in the face of manifold negativities. There is only You to guard me."

This eminent personality did not have anything to do with sin even in his dreams. I do not know what he was referring to with "sin" and with reference to which condition of his he is moaning with woes like that! If only a drop of these considerations were to be found in degenerate ones like us who are under the burden of so many sins!

At another time, he was turning to the door of the Munificent and was petitioning thus with profound self-criticism:

> "My God, my mistakes are so gross and so many, but Your forgiveness and magnanimity is greater. I will try to be loyal to my promise to You; and You please grant a look to this miserable servant of Yours with the ampleness of Your mercy, for I regret so much of what I committed!"

I wonder what mistake the conqueror of Khaybar made for which he is sighing here with regret. And he would continue:

"My God! Save this slave from Your wrath and retribution who is at Your door with the collar of servitude, in expectation of Your Glorified Countenance!"

May my soul be sacrificed for Ali who calls himself a slave; may the Compassionate Lord let us people who are virtually deaf and blind to have such profound self-criticism also! The noble Messenger's son-in-law continued opening up to God as follows:

"If you do not hold me by the hand, O God, I will perish; but if you guard me, then I will not fall forever!"

Nobody has ever seen you fall; if your words are meant to be a lesson to us, then we welcome them, knowing that it isn't relevant to your person.

At another time, the following pearls came out of his tongue fully spirited with feelings of awe and fearful reverence before God's grandeur:

"My God, if You will only forgive those of perfect goodness, then what will happen to those who follow their fancies and stagger their way on, who is going to forgive them? O Lord, if I have gone astray from the way of piety, here I am in Your presence. Remorse in my heart, and repentance in my tongue, please forgive this slave of Yours! When I remember Your favors, my fears melt away like ice; and when my sins charge at me, my eyes fill with tears!"

My dear sultan, you always cried and never laughed; you never knew anything as worldliness, and strictly never bowed before the carnal soul. If this petition is aimed to awaken people like us so we can be human in the true sense of the word, then we salute it. But unfortunately, we buried those virtues in the cemetery of indolence long ago, and we are creeping our way in the valleys of affectation. Here is another prayer of his at God's door, his head humbly down:

"If I am to be sent away from Your court and depraved of Your special graces, then from whom else can I hope for forgiveness and mercy?"

Oh, Ali! The world always saw you as a brilliant mirror to the Divine, and with God's permission, they always knew you as a hero of compassion.

As one of the closest of those closest to God, these breaths should be an expression of his refined and profound considerations that go beyond our horizons of cognition; unfortunately, we have been distant from such noble considerations for centuries. If only these entreaties, which go on and on across heavenly horizons of angels, could mean something to the dark souls of ourselves with darkened hearts!

Even a tenth of such feelings of awe and reverence before the grandeur of God is unfortunately not found in certain leaders and degenerate ones in our time. God knows that there is an abundance of people who live in such a carefree fashion, as if they have already received their certificate of salvation. Unfortunate ones detached from God and dizzied with worldly pomp and ostentation are beyond count. Their hearts are dead. Lies, defamation, and vices are the most common commodities among them.

The world and its temptations dominate over feelings of the Afterlife. In terms of religion and belief, every land is in need of intensive care, for they have become institutions of affectation and formality. Mephisto has dealt a deadly blow to Faust once again, and he has done so by using religious values. It appears that a new revival has been postponed to a future spring. Those looking forward to a true dawn are on the verge of despair.

We want to maintain our hopes of a fresh revival; but what we see before our eyes are a huge deformation, candles of hope losing their light, and heroes who will breathe life into this dead world under lethal pressure. Those who applaud darkness are beyond count. There are heaps of troubles, and cures are only imaginary. Right and wrong are intertwined and masses lack common sense.

How strange a time we have reached

Who is brave, who is not, we cannot tell.

Everybody is seeking a cure for their wound

What is the cure, what is the trouble, we cannot tell.

Ruhsati

It is understood that what falls to those who have some share of being human is to say, *"So the proper recourse for us is a becoming patience"* (Yusuf 12:18). They need to read the times and the generation correctly. They need to wait for the dawning of "the mystery of God's absolute Oneness in the light of Divine Unity."

May the Almighty Reviver, Whose mercy is dominant over His wrath, not let people experience any further disappointments! Amin.

FACING THE SELF – THE SUCCESSORS

So much so a source of blessings was Prophet Muhammad, peace be upon him, that he always had followers who embodied the same spirit and devotion. Those who had the opportunity to be close to him and witness his person with their eyes and hearts lived in a constant state of rapture with this delight. They walked in his footsteps with the excitement of being imbued with that state, and they always made sure this path that led to him was filled with travelers. Hundreds of thousands have taken wing towards him, their eyes always eagerly fixed on this first "circle," (the leading Companions of the Prophet) and their hearts willing to behold what lies beyond. Watchful for the furthest horizons, they have taught the manners of this journey to those who staggered on their way.

For those who are on this path, faith in God (*iman*) is a lively source of excitement in hearts. Knowledge (*marifa*) and love of God (*mahabba*) are each a sparkling torch in feelings and thoughts. Their eagerness to meet the real owner of everything sheds light on their journey to eternity. They have walked without falter to the beyond with eagerness for reunion with God (*liqa'ullah*), which is a never-fading source of energy in feelings and thoughts; their hearts always beating with the excitement of beholding the very horizons of those in the first circle. They ran on the same path with them without fatigue, and they do so with an insightful perspective of what they saw, with a resolution for journeying in the realms beyond the horizons by means of their "mechanism of conscience,"[1] their hearts permeated with the awe of this state and the entirety of their physical and spiritual anatomy in full resonance.

With deep faith and knowledge, they are thoroughly equipped in both material and spiritual sense. They leave behind worldliness and materialism entirely. They disregard dirty urges of the carnal soul and its temptations. Though they soar in heavenly realms, their hearts still quiver in fear. They keep wailing and groaning as if they were the sinful ones in this world. They question themselves with the deepest concerns day and night, and they always have considerations as expressed in:

If the All-Merciful One weighs my sins as they are,
I fear the scales on the Day of Judgment will break.

They keep sighing night and day out of fear, as if they have committed some wrongdoing despite their already glorious spiritual rank. Humility is at the core of their existence. They feel disgusted by receiving appreciation and applause. They abhor glory, prestige, and pomp. They always behave as an ordinary person among other people. Acknowledging that all goodness, achievements, and extraordinary qualities come from their Creator, bowing is no more enough for them to show their gratitude, they go down to prostration in reverence.

A slave as I am, I am not worthy of this gift
Why am I being granted this favor?

M. Lütfi

With these feelings, they continue to be relentless in their self-criticism, and are immersed in expressions of humility and self-effacement. They adopt the following important principle of the Qur'an as a part of their character: "*(O human being!) Whatever good happens to you, it is from God; and whatever evil befalls you, it is from yourself*" (an-Nisa 4:79). They do not forget their single mistake or lapse which weighs so

---

1   Human conscience, according to Bediüzzaman Said Nursi, is a combination of the following faculties: spiritual heart (*latifa al-rabbaniya*), willpower (*irada*), consciousness, and feelings. Fethullah Gülen calls this combination "mechanism of conscience."

heavily on their shoulders, even after many years. They forget or disregard the good things they have made or accomplished, which may have helped thousands of people. Even if the thought of crediting themselves for a dazzling accomplishment or triumph crosses their minds, they dismiss such thoughts and acknowledge all success to be from God as a grace for people's collective work and solidarity. These are the character traits of the devoted souls walking on the path of the All-Truthful One, and such is the constant state of monumental personages whose hearts are completely oriented with the ones in the first circle, seeking God's approval.

Now, with my broken statements, I wish to narrate examples of "facing the self" from some loyal servants of God, whose eyes and hearts were with the members of the circle. My words can only represent a few drops from their immense ocean.

Zayn al-Abidin

As one of the radiant fruits of the blessed tree of the Prophet's family, Imam Zayn al-Abidin was a person of sublime virtues. His father was Husayn (the Prophet's grandson), his grandmother was Fatima (the Prophet's daughter), and his grandfather was Ali, the prince of the chivalrous (*futuwwa*), and his great grandfather was the noble Prophet (pbuh). Zayn al-Abidin was a fortunate person who opened his eyes to the world in such a bright ethos and flourished with heavenly water of life, had his heart and spirit always set on God so much so that his path never ever crossed sins even in his dreams. Wherever he turned his eyes, he was enraptured by a view of the first circle. He kept soaring high towards that blessed source of inspiration with a desire and eagerness of reunion with his noble family.

Permeated with such feelings and thoughts, he always desired and aimed to be on that blessed course. Always in devotion to the Divine, he assigned no worth to himself, and constantly engaged in self-effacement, a state of being which Seyyid Nigari describes in his own way as follows:

Can one who seeks the Beloved care about their own soul?

Can one caring for their own soul be concerned for the Beloved?

And thus Zayn al-Abidin kept seeking God and completely closed his eyes to all else, because he was in a state of constant exposure to the first circle, physically and spiritually. His heart would beat with the excitement of being under the same light with them, and he would live with a zest for servanthood to God. Among his prayers constantly offered are the following supplications, which I will do my best to convey here, but will do so by focusing more on the meaning rather than the exact wording; I will not constrain myself to verbal limitations. Instead of rendering all his supplications here in full, what follows is his heartbreaking cries, which I occasionally interpolate with short phrases to offer my personal take on some of his words, hoping that his inner sighs are better internalized first by myself and others like me:

> "My God! The wrongs and sins I have been committing have put a mantle of abasement on my soul. By remaining apart from You, I have found myself in a state of poverty" [*O Imam, have you ever been apart? F.G.*]. "The gigantic wrongs that I have committed have darkened my heart" [*No, a hundred thousand times no! F.G.*]. "I seek refuge in You, God Almighty, my only Besought and Beloved! Please accept me as I turn to Your door with sincere repentance, and bless me with a fresh revival as if I have been revived after death" [*If you are not alive, then what should we call ourselves, the unfortunate "walking dead," like myself! How should we pray, while you are praying like this! F.G.*]. "I swear I never knew anyone but You Who could care for my wounds and heal my troubles, and in spite of everything, here I submissively expect to be forgiven in Your presence. If you expel this slave of Yours, which door can I ever turn to and with whom can I ever seek refuge? If I am expelled from that door, I will utterly be in a pitiable and shameful condition!"

Oh, dear Imam Abidin, we have studied you and others like you in the literature of the Prophet's life, and have come to recognize you with your humility and heartfelt supplications. If the cause of your wailing is the temporary fog that occasionally seeps into your imagination, if this is the factor that triggers your pains, how fortunate you are. And how pitiable are unfortunate ones of our time such as myself who live their entire lives in that fog and smoke, and the so-called theologians[2] who assume themselves to be religious!

Zayn al-Abidin does not suffice with the above prayers. Below he opens another page in his compositions of wails:

> "O the Exalted Lord, Who even forgives the greatest sins and embraces stricken hearts with compassion! I wish and beg You to pardon my disgracing sins and hide away my shameful wrongs and forgive this slave of Yours in the warm atmosphere of Your forgiveness, along with those whom You saved with Your clemency and mercy."

I wish it was possible to find at least a hundredth of these wailings in the spiritual world of those who spend their life in places of worship, who put on airs in Sufi lodges, who waste their lives in nests of heedlessness appearing to be religious schools, and those so-called believers whose faith does not pass beyond imitation and who spend their lives in self-glorification saying "I did this, I did that."

Zayn al-Abidin continues to open up to God, his yearnings now reaching a peak:

> "If repentance and penitence are titles for a heartfelt remorse, so I swear I repent a thousand times for all I committed! If asking forgiveness from You is a means of being absolved from sins, so I cry with truly heartfelt remorse and wish You to forgive this poor servant of Yours!"

With my full respect to him, I skip some of his expressions of sigh and wailing and jump to the following one:

> "O God! You are the One Who has opened wide the gates of sincere repentance for Your servants and informed us with this good news. You decree "*O you who believe! Turn to God in sincere and reforming repentance*" (at-Tahrim 66:8) and thus summon us to the chamber of Your Oneness. Those who turn to this door You have opened will hopefully find what they expect, as a result of Your grace. Sins and wrongs certainly are not becoming for servants, but there is no doubt that You are so magnanimous at forgiveness and clemency."

---

2   By "so-called theologians," Gülen makes a reference to certain scholars of theology who compromise values of faith in return for status or money.

Let us add the following to that:

> *Bestow Your graces, O my Sovereign,*
>
> *do not deprive the needy and destitute from Your grace;*
>
> *Does it befit the All-Munificent One to stop sending graces to His servants?*
>
> M. Lütfi

Yearning souls always presented their petition with this gist of imploring, which, if it will not be disrespectful against the Almighty, I also favor in my own life.

Zayn al-Abidin voiced his woeful sighs, hoping to gain God's forgiveness and mercy. Here is more from his pearl-like prayers:

> "O God, I am not the first person that has spent his life in rebellion and then turned to You with a sincere feeling of remorse. I have touched the doorknob of Your door of Mercy, and thus expected Your mercy, compassion, and grace; so many others bowed their heads before that door and none of them returned empty-handed. O my Most Exalted Lord! I have come to Your Sublime Presence without any provisions; You are such a magnanimous Bestower; please respond to my prayers and implorations, and do not let me down in my hopes and expectations!"

These sighs and pleas resonate with those made by the people within the blessed first circle. Thus, they offer these compositions of prayer from their heart to those whose hearts gave in to heedlessness and are astray from the course that they are supposed to take. Their goal with these heart-piercing prayers is to try and make the souls of those stranded on the path – like myself – feel what they felt. With lyrics from the blessed first circle around the Prophet, and the tune from the angelic soul of Zayn al-Abidin, who burned with love of God, they express their supplications in the tune of a call to prayer, and attempt to come to grips with their soul through prayers such as:

> *Sleeping heedlessly is not appropriate for the humble servant,*
>
> *When the All-Beneficent calls out with compassion at nights.*
>
> İbrahim Hakkı

Such prayers resonate with the heartstrings of those who understand and – if they are not dead spiritually – rise and come running with
the hopes of getting closer to the Almighty. May God enable us, too, to
be awakened with those sincere invocations and come to our senses!

Zayn al-Abidin does not suffice only with opening up to God, and
thus wishes to turn to Him in every way that he can spiritually. To be of
guidance to those coming from behind in how to face oneself for sincere
repentance, he places his head down at the door of Divine beneficence
and mercy, and this time offers a different prayer:

> "My God! My wrongdoings and sins enshroud my soul with despi-
> cableness" [*As if he were someone who ever committed sin. F.G.*]. "I
> have become separate from You, and I am clad in misery. Sins have
> utterly darkened my heart. I am at Your door, my head bowing on
> the doorstep of Your majesty; O the Solely Worshiped and Besought
> One! Please do accept this beseeching and repentance of mine! Once
> more, I have turned to Your Most Exalted Court. With my head
> humbly bowed down, I obediently stand in Your Supreme Presence
> and wait for a decree of my forgiveness. If you expel this servant of
> Yours from Your door, whom can I turn to; whom can I seek refuge
> with! O Almighty Lord, Who forgives even the greatest sins and
> dresses up injured hearts in disorientation. I beg from You to forgive
> my shameful wrongs and regard them as null, and to veil all of my
> sins. In the realms beyond, do not deprive me either, of Your graces
> to those whom You love and of that refreshing climate of Your favors,
> bounty, and beneficence!"

By presenting one more different picture of imploration with these
words, he attempts to drink from the fountains of forgiveness, repentance,
and sincere penitence. In direct proportion with their vast horizons of
spiritual knowledge, they grieve so deeply that it would be easy to mistake
them for sinners. Even though we may not be aware, such sighs are in
fact prayers of glorification and actually belong to the horizons of those
closest to God; they are like a call to prayer to awaken the unawares. No
matter what a person of such caliber who annihilated himself in the way
and love of God says, I think he did not even engage with evil temptations
even in his dream. Nevertheless, he still kept praying and asking for for-

giveness, which was an outcome of his exceptionally close position before God; this is a lesson and serves as spiritual counsel for us.

"I am at Your doorstep," says Zayn al-Abidin constantly and keeps petitioning God with his head humbly bowed down:

> "O my exalted God! Do not ever let me be separated from You and fall into sin. Do not allow me to drift into rebellion, which is like an all-consuming sea. Save this servant of Yours from drifting to things to incur Your displeasure! Here I complain to You about my distressing carnal soul which makes me run after never ending worldly ambitions; my carnal soul that keeps whining against troubles and misfortunes, which credits itself for every good thing and is always inclined to futility. Inflicted with heedlessness and oblivion, my carnal soul makes me ever prone to sins, and tempts me to delay my repentance to You with each passing day."

I do not know what this pure and innocent soul, who already rests on the horizons of contentment with God, means by his "carnal soul." He goes even further seeking refuge against Satan and whirlpools of fancies:

> "O God! I complain to You about this dead heart of mine, captivated by various evil whisperings and hardened with rust, and which forgot the meaning of being in fear and awe of God."

Can they make sense of these prayers, those among us who has been in oblivion of tears and shudders of the heart now for centuries, those who have reduced faith to outward rituals, those who are described in the Qur'an (al-Jumu'ah 62:5) as "donkeys loaded with books," those who are not aware of what they are carrying?

Zayn al-Abidin still does not suffice with this and turns to the horizons of awe and reverence of God, and to the essential elements of human perfection and virtue in the shade of the truth, "awe of God is the beginning of wisdom." He implores, as if voicing the following lines, and once more he humbly bends over before God, the All-Truth:

> *It is neither knowledge nor conscience that elevates character*
> *It is reverence to God that evokes the sense of virtue in people*
>
> *If fear of the Almighty in hearts were to disappear,*

Wisdom or the conscience would not have any influence anymore

Life would fall to an animal level; no, even lower than animals!

M. Akif

This is the thinking of Zayn al-Abidin and with such thoughts he inspires others to become true humans. He expresses these feelings through prayers of reverence before God. He laments like a reed flute in a state even further beyond the peaks of consciousness of being seen by Him; he is in a unique mode of vigilance as if in the Divine presence. Here are a few bunches of fear and awe from him in different patterns and hues of hope:

"O my Exalted God, the Eternal Sovereign of mercy and compassion! Are You to throw this loyal servant of Yours who turned to You into the fire of being without You? Are You to deprive me of Your forgiveness and not pardon this helpless one whose misdeeds can only be purified by Your immense ocean of mercy? No, a hundred thousand times no, of course! You never let down in disappointment those who turned to Your Divine court."

As if he remained breathless here, his heart resonates with the strike of a plectrum of awe:

"If only I could know that You included my name in the book of fortunate ones and honored me with Your closeness! If I only knew this, so that my eyes and heart too would light up with joy. O God! Do not shut Your gates of Mercy against those who know You and believe in You even only to some extent! As I hope and believe, please do not let down the hearts You have revived by letting them feel Your exalted existence into the misery of being without You—You never did so—and thus do not let us down into the fires of separation and Hell! My God! Save me, Your servant from Your displeasure and due sufferings!"

One can feel his deep concerns in the following words:

"Save me from the torment of Hell on that toughest day when good and evil will be distinguished, when people will be at their wits' end, when souls engaged in good acts will be enraptured with the rejoice of closeness to God, when unfortunate ones who misspent their lives will shake with the grief of remoteness, and when nobody will be subjected to the slightest degree of injustice."

With the feelings of an utterly sinful one Zayn al-Abidin sets about most heartfelt implorations. With the awareness that *"two fears and two assurances"*[3] do not coexist, he passes from one petitioning to another. He constantly implores God with his open hands at the door of His Mercy and teaches those who are believers on the outside, but not on the inside, and those who are deprived of awe and reverence of God.

Together with all of the fears and worries in his entreaties, Zayn al-Abidin does not neglect to petition God with reference to Divine beneficence, and as he does that his heart changes rhythm with the excitement of hope. By behaving in this way, he presents an attitude that calls to mind the act of straightening up after bowing to God. For those who continue to struggle spiritually, he thus points to the ampleness of Divine Mercy with reference to the fact that *God's mercy prevails over His wrath.*[4]

What would happen even if my sins were like the mount Qaf,

O Majestic One,

Compared to Your sea of mercy, it is surely a little thing.

Laedri

He acts in accordance with this poetic idiom and spits in the face of sins and faults by imploring, "Please hold my hand to guidance, O God!" After he places his head down on the doorstep of hope and petitions for mercy, he enters in a mood as if he were inhaling fresh oxygen and sighs on. Here are a few droplets from those breaths:

3   In a *hadith qudsi*, the Prophet reported from Almighty the following: "By My might, I will not combine two fears or two assurances upon My servant. If he fears Me in the world, I will assure his protection on the Day of Resurrection. If he felt safe from Me in the world, he will fear Me on the Day of Resurrection" (*Sahih Ibn Hibban*, 640).

4   Bukhari, *Tawhid*, 22; Muslim, *Tawba*, 15.

"O the One Who responds with mercy as soon as His servants turn to Him, Who never leaves their hopes unanswered, Who saves them from the grief of falling apart from Him with the extra ways and disciplines that make them closer to Him, Who covers up the defects of those polluted with sins and vices! O my Most Exalted Lord! As You never turned down those who turned to Your door with hope and placed their head on Your doorstep empty handed, do not abandon this humble servant of Yours to despair either!"

With these cries, Zayn al-Abidin makes petitions in the axis of hope (*raja*) and fear (*hawf*), and as he does so he signals the successors of his path to turn to that door inclined towards hope. For those who have lost their sense of direction, his petitions show them where to turn to and let the vastness of Divine mercy be heard, even by unfortunate ones. He calls to them to share his experiences and to hopefully inspire them to find their way. By presenting them with the most vivid messages woven out of hope and fear, he shows the ways towards a fresh revival with lyrics of resurrection after death; afterwards, like the Archangel Israfil's breath to initiate the resurrection, he blows life into them and turns them to the direction of the Divine they lost.

This chapter could go on and on, but, with apologies to Zayn al-Abidin and to readers, I would like to move from these diamond-like considerations at this point to another set of petitions unique to his spirit; a spirit whose anatomy is established on heavenly riches. These are his life-giving angelic melodies which he uttered while his tears streamed on, his tongue guided by the heart, his thoughts beyond metaphysical realms, his *sir* (an inner spiritual faculty, *secret*) in citadels even further beyond, surpassing our comprehension. Here are a few droplets, or rather "legend of the spirit," by Zayn al-Abidin:

"My God! Though I am without provisions, my reliance and submission to You are complete. Despite this, when I think that my transgressions are boundless, I shake and fear from being subjected to Your punishment. By contrast, when the ampleness of Your mercy comes to my view, my heart overflows with a feeling of optimism. In that mood, although my sins make me lament with fear about perdition, my hope about Your pardoning gives signals of possible forgiveness to my soul."

What a balanced approach, which is found in those closest to God! What a profound blend of hope and fear! He continues to say:

> "Even though I came to Your sublime presence empty-handed, the consideration of the ampleness of Your bountifulness reinvigorates this servant of Yours and my eyes start shining brightly with Your beneficence's promise of benisons. So much so that at the same moment when I am brimful with transgressions, my heart begins to experience changes of rhythm one after the other, with extra surprises of Your pardoning and breezes of proximity. Here I am in Your presence, O God! I let myself to the waterfalls of Your mercy and get away from myself as far as I can and turn to You with the entirety of my being!"

Fear on one hand, hope on the other, Zayn al-Abidin prays on with an acceptance to have not been able to live up to the lofty status he posits himself in his relationship with God Almighty. Then this towering figure from those closest to God changes his orbit of prayer; he once more takes into consideration the shower of Divine blessings he had already received and begins to resonate with thankfulness by putting his face down onto the doorstep of gratitude. This is similar to how Bediüzzaman describes the purpose of worship: "Worship is not preliminary to future rewards, but a result to blessings that are already given."[5] He responds to God's blessings beyond count and measure with thankful praises by assigning his tongue and lips under the command of his heart:

> "My God! I do not know what to say before Your immense blessings that come showering on the horizons of my perception consecutively. Before the Divine favors out of Your grace and generosity I remain spellbound and lost for words. I consider Your very special blessings that come flowing like waterfalls and much beyond my deserts under the light of 'Were you to attempt to count God's blessings, you could not reckon them' (Ibrahim 14:34). Helpless to say anything, I am humbled with indebtedness before those special bestowals of Yours, like

---

5   The Twenty-Fourth Word, Fifth Branch. Hüseyin Akarsu's translation reads as follows: "Worship of God is not an act through which to demand a Divine reward in the future, but rather the necessary result of a past Divine favor."

my revival with faith, turning to Your door via Islam, honored with servanthood only to You and my head down on the doorstep of Your munificence and grace, my hand on the knob of beneficence and bestowals, upon which I say *'all of these are from You'* (an-Nisa 4:78) and feel revitalized with thankfulness. Actually, even this feeling of thankfulness is from You. Whenever I offer thanks to You, given that thankfulness is another blessing of Yours – with such a virtuous cycle of thankfulness, I will never be able to offer due praise and thanks to You."

If only we could continue our lives always on this course with awareness of these bestowals! Although we are not capable of thorough comprehension, I wish we could take what God has given as a sign of what He will give and thus take up the path to eternal bliss. It is important not to let our hearts fall for this transient world, which is compared to a "carcass." If only we could have turned our backs to worldly status, fame, glory, wealth, corporeal desires, and thus turned to the Almighty God without faltering. Alas! We fell for such attractions! With delusions of immortality, we have been entangled with worldly ambitions assuming they would last forever and suffered losses we could have won. Bediüzzaman puts it so beautifully: "Alas! We have been deceived. We thought that this worldly life is constant, and thus utterly wasted all of it. Indeed, this passing life is but a sleep that passed like a dream. This life, having no foundation, flies like the wind."[6]

It is such a bitter fact that we fell for this deception, and at the expense of losing eternity. We were captivated by the passing attractions of this world, condemned eternal realms to oblivion, and thus darkened our futures. So much so that we have neither been thankful enough for the Divine bestowals and benisons, nor have we been able to understand that the real life is not the one we have today, but the one that will come tomorrow, the one all these blessings are meant to be used for. To put this in the breaths of Ziya Paşa:

> Alas, we are the losers of this game once again;
> The loss is obvious, but I don't know if we won anything at all.

6   The Seventeenth Word, Second Station.

Actually, it was not possible for us to win. Because we have led a carefree life as if we would never die and rendered this world—which is created as an arable field for the Afterlife—into a wasteland. By destroying the bridges extending to eternity one by one, we have ceased thinking of belief for the realms beyond. We have not managed to come to our senses to see our miserable condition and turn to God.

With his head humbly lowered at the doorstep of Divine beneficence, and the eye of his heart watchful at that ajar door expecting that his care will be responded with care, Zayn al-Abidin voices another petition while the rhythm of his heart beats with the name of God. He presents such compositions of loyalty and integrity to the Almighty that those closest to him listen with ears filled with admiration:

> "O my Sustainer! Various imaginings of doubts keep roiling within me. They befog the heavenly purity of Your perfectly wholesome bestowals. Please eliminate the fog and smoke of doubts and my considerations unbecoming for a servant, which are obstacles in the path of closeness to You! Let my heart overflow with the feeling of begging and imploring You! Let my heart always be truly revived with the discernment and consciousness of feeling close to You!"

He trembles like a leaf even with just one percent probability of experiencing a lapse; all faculties of his brain are full of this meaning, as was expressed by one humble servant[7]:

> *My head laid down on the sill of Your Mercy,*
>
> *Turned my face to You, enraptured.*
>
> *As a sinful slave with a tainted face,*
>
> *I am at Your command.*

With tunes of faithfulness, Zayn al-Abidin opens up to the Creator and waits for an edict of salvation, as he always did. He does not suffice with knocking on the door of Divine mercy and intercession with these wails of obedience and submission, but he yearns for perfect faith and righteous deeds. He goes on to crown his entreaties with horizons of sin-

---

7   A poem by Fethullah Gülen.

cerity by seeking God's good pleasure:

"O My Compassionate Sustainer! Make us among those who seek to make You well pleased and who keep endeavoring for this sake! Bestow the honor of devoted worship in Your sublime presence, which is a means of Your intimate grace—on these powerless servants of Yours, who have their eyes constantly on Your door and their hands on that doorknob, cherishing thoughts—of what they regard as the greatest grace—of gaining Your good pleasure, with zealous love and heartfelt dreams... those whom You honored with different conferrals in Your presence; those whom You blessed with attainments beyond imagination; those whom You allow to perceive You, out of Your grace and generosity. Make us from among those distinguished servants whose love and attachment You crowned with superb zeal, and whose consciences You blessed with Self-disclosure; make us from among Your distinguished servants whose hearts You directed to Yourself with love and ardor every moment. O the Beneficent One Who does not let His loyal servants down, who do not get enough of turning to Yourself, seeking Your good pleasure! Include this servant of Yours among the fortunate ones whose prayers are acceptable!"

Oh, Zayn al-Abidin! A luminous soul who is so dear, and whose face is always turned towards that sublime circle around the Messenger! You constantly asked God for the same blessings and consistently made these prayers internally all the time. Your voice and the voice of others like you have traveled across time and have reached even our era. Many whose hearts were ready for your implorations, voiced similar prayers from their conscience, with their hands on the same doorknob. This is how they opened up to God, to the One Who never turned down those who appealed to Him with love and attachment, and He never let them suffer separation.

The blessed imam Zayn al-Abidin deepens his imploration further and begs earnestly as follows:

"*O My Compassionate Sustainer!* Please be my comforter! Please eliminate the desolation of being without You in my soul. Forgive me for having lapses and having staggered while on my journey through life. Please cover my wrongdoings with Your Divine Name, 'the All-

Veiler' (*al-Sattar*). By taking this servant of Yours in sanctuaries of protection, bless him with Your special reassurance, please!"

By saying so, he cherishes expectations of Divine succor, providence, guardianship, and grace, and holds on tight to that "*firm, unbreakable handle*" (al-Baqara 2:256), thus he soars toward transcending physical space with the wings of reliance, submission, and commitment to Him.

Still, Zayn al-Abidin finds himself unsatisfied even after spending every opportunity to surge upwards to the Infinite, he turns to the sanctum of love and sets about begging for love from the True Beloved. He says "more!" and flaps his wings onward, thus ascending to the horizons beyond and even further beyond. On the way to the peak he aims to reach, there remains no Divine Attributes and States he does not turn to. With genuine humbleness like a beggar, he dyes his petitions with the hue of Divine Names. He constantly follows the examples of Prophet Jacob and Jonah, and whispers with sincerity "*I only disclose my anguish and sorrow to God*" (Yusuf 12:86) and keeps waiting at the door of the Resolver of Troubles in a concerned and touching condition. He continues to pray and present the finest compositions of supplication to the Almighty One.

From time to time, he is filled with the feeling of hope for God's grace, mercy, and with the joyful zeal of gratitude, which can be best characterized in the words of Yunus Emre:

> *Whatever comes from You is good for me*
>
> *Be it a cape, or a shroud,*
>
> *A fresh rose, or a thorn*
>
> *Good is Your grace, good is Your wrath*

With hopes imbued with contentedness, he reveres each blessed inspiration as special treatment from his Sustainer. He welcomes all of these words and occurrences he regards as Divine presents with joy.

This was the way that those that were imbued with the hue of the blessed "circle" had always felt and existed; with a never-subsiding sense of excitement, determination, and perseverance. Their dizzying heavenliness made angels envious and drove devils away. Rumi, the polar star of those intoxicated with love of God, narrates the human condition so well in the following line: "There are times when angels admire us; and there are times when even devils hate our crudeness." The bright personages described in the first part of this line are those like Zayn al-Abidin who are always navigated to the blessed "circle."

Today, how many people are there who make dwellers of the heavens envious? It is as clear as day, however, that people who make the Devil dance with joy outnumbers any other era. I pray that the All-Compassionate One will save our contemporaries that have been led astray by Satan, and that God lets them experience spiritual revivals by allowing them to walk in the footsteps of the "masters of the heart" who are directed to the blessed "circle."

Uways al-Qarni

Uways al-Qarni – an illustrious personage so assiduous at faith and at his relationship with God; one of those closest to the Almighty (*aqrab al muqarrabin*). He was a contemporary of the "age of light" – the time of the Prophet. He saw what needed to be seen and was able to attend the circles of the blessed Companions of the Prophet. He was a person of the most fortunate kind who, despite himself being born in the next generation (*tabi'un*), was side by side with the first generation of believers (*ashab*). His connection with the Almighty and His Messenger was thorough. With respect to his heaven-bound spiritual progress, he was in line with those in the blessed "circle." Uways was held back by his mother's demand, but he truly was a person imbued with the hue of that circle and a brilliant personage of his own kind.[8] Although he had heard the call, he could not be a Companion to the Prophet, by meeting him physically. Thanks to his perseverance and speed to let his heart and spirit flourish, he became a saintly figure recognized by all; he received much esteem from the early caliphs, and he enjoyed a spiritual position on a par with the Companions.

---

8   Uways made a visit to see the Prophet (pbuh) but could not find him in place.
     Complying with his mother's demand, he returned home without waiting, unable
     to meet the Prophet.

Uways was so closely connected with the blessed circle that he was able to sense what was otherwise beyond perception and acquire everything to be acquired in their atmosphere that radiated from the Prophet. He conveyed to others as much knowledge as he received and also shed light on the path of hundreds of others to realize their spiritual potential. He lived to revive others spiritually and he always had the excitement of letting them feel the Divine as he did. While being mentioned so honorably by others, he constantly kept up an attitude of humility and modesty that was utterly unsympathetic to taking pride. With his touching supplications, he always inspired solemn God-consciousness. Although we estimate that sins could not taint even his imagination, as a requirement of his special attainments, he overstated the pettiest "fog" and "smoke" as gigantic evils that he had committed and sighed with concern, an outcome of his spiritual excellence.

Here are a few of his heart-rending tunes that perfectly correspond the sincere supplications of his predecessors; or rather, a few priceless drops that are worth oceans, each no different than a breath of an angel, offered with a solemnity similar to those closest to God Almighty:

"O my Most High Sustainer! With reliance on and submission to You, here I beg for Your help. Neither in this world nor in the next, do not leave me on my own with my impotence, poverty, and nothingness! O the Eternal Monarch of these days, tomorrows, and of all times, the Compassionate Sustainer! As a sinful servant of Yours, here I am at Your door of Mercy, with my impoverished state!"

Oh, Uways, the blessed soul! If you are impoverished as you say in prayer, I don't know what the miserable servants of our time should call themselves! I am not able to say anything, but the wise Bediüzzaman referred to such people as "the unfortunate walking dead." He should be right at that. Uways implores further:

"I am weak, slovenly, abased, a captive of Yours, and a bankrupt helpless one; whereas You are the Sovereign of sovereigns. You answer the demands of those who turn to Your door with the ampleness of Your Mercy! I am overwhelmed with my worry and sorrow, but I am before the court of the All-Generous One Who fulfills requests of those with worried hearts who stagger their way on. My transgressions are beyond count! With the hope of being included among Your favorite and distinguished servants, my head is humbly at the doorstep of Your mercy, and I knock that door hoping to be forgiven."

I wonder what he means by "transgression." O Uways, the saintly sultan of spiritual faculties who made his predecessors envy his profundity of heart and spirit. While your contemporaries and your environment saw you as an exemplar and showered you with much appreciation, is this supplication of yours a form of self-criticism as befits your vast horizons, or is it a lesson of being directed to their sanctuaries for disoriented servants like myself who are scattered here and there like prayer beads out of their string? Uways continues:

> "With due embarrassment and excitement about my faults, I turn to Your Chamber of forgiveness, my face humbly down with the hope of forgiveness and say, O my Gracious Lord! As a wretched soul who wronged himself, my eyes are on the door of Your ample mercy, expecting that it will open, and my heart eager to be showered with Your special graces, I am expecting what is to be expected from You. Though my offenses are beyond count, here I push aside whatever I have as my own eligibility, I seek refuge in Your Mercy that makes anyone eligible, and I am expecting Your special favors while looking downwards contritely."

> "My Almighty God, with my innumerable wrongs and awareness of there being no other doors to turn to, I intend to stay eternally if need be before Your door of mercy, which is ever open to everyone."

> "My God! I turn to You once more with these countless and unending transgressions of mine, for I do not know any other doors to turn to. O my Almighty God! You are the Supremely Exalted and Beneficent One, whereas I am a servant of the humblest kind. If You do not have mercy on this wretched servant of Yours, who else can ever help him? O my Eternal Sultan, my Ultimate Refuge! You are the True Owner of everything and everyone, and this one at Your door is just an ordinary servant. If You do not favor him and take him to Your hand of Munificence, who else can ever support him? O my Ultimate

Provider of shelter and support! You are the Absolute Owner of glory, while this poor one is so lowly; if You do not hold him by the hand, who else can save him from this abject state?"

Oh, Uways, paragon of perfection and light of my eye, if you are lowly, tell me how we can name our own situation.

"My Lord! You are such an exalted All-Compassionate One that You keep Your gates of forgiveness wide open even for pitch-black souls who have committed some of the gravest sins, and You let our hopes soar with the glad tidings of, *'turn to God all together in repentance...'* (an-Nur 24:31). Please do not send away from that door this lowly poor servant who spent his life tainted with transgressions!"

"O All-Caring and Favoring, the One Who supports everyone with His Endless mercy and compassion and fills them with relief! I am another helpless servant of Yours, who staggers his way on; I seek refuge in the vastness of Your Mercy against the darkness and narrowness of the grave and hardness of the decreed judgment, and here I beg and implore for Your mercy."

I wonder whether we ever opened up to God this way, be it once, with these profound considerations. I don't think so! Every time he remembers the fearsome states beyond the grave, Uways prays with such pleas for mercy:

"Do not deprive this fallen one of Your providence and grace when I will give account of my life to the interrogating angels! I will ask for Your mercy and hope for Your clemency and compassion against all pressures and assaults I face. I will cry out, 'mercy please!' against the narrowness and darkness of the grave. Against the dreadful states when people frantically tremble not knowing whether they will be taken under Your protection or not, 'mercy, please mercy!'"

"Mercy, please mercy, when the earth shakes continuously and the ground turns to dust and smoke, when mountains burst into the air like carded wool, the skies rolled up, and the earth and the heavens are overturned with successive changes; during that difficult Judgment Day when everybody will be resurrected and gathered before the Divine Presence. Mercy, please mercy, before those dreadful scenes when everybody, people and jinn, will be faced with their deeds; during those grunts of remorse when those who spent their lives in unbelief and misguidance will lament 'wishing to turn to dust.'[9] Mercy, please mercy, when those who spent their worldly lives in valleys of rebellion and a swamp of sins are brought to account."

By saying these, that monumental personage whose innocence was confirmed by all accounts went through vast amounts of supplication. He would live with these night and day. His tongue and lips wept under the command of the heart all the time. As Uways breathed in and out with such considerations, breezes of revival with the pattern of the blessed Age of Light – the time of the Prophet – were blowing around him. The exhausted would feel resuscitated with these heartfelt laments; imagining what is portrayed in these prayers they'd sharpen their spiritual perceptions with an amplified wisdom. They would form a chorus of prayer, thanks to that heavenly tune.

If only one tenth of such feelings, thoughts, and imagination were found in those who claim to be believers in our time! If only homes would be revived in heart and spirit with the mood brought by imagining these otherworldly scenes and joined voices with those imploring petitions. If only establishments of religious education did not remain indifferent to these heartfelt entreaties. If only sermons and addresses could be freed of the influence of mundane life and that they were part of the melody of these prayers! It is such a bitter fact that in our time, homes, social environment, centers of guidance, and even some spiritual orders are polluted with the latest gossip. The spirit of family homes is hospitalized; establishments of knowledge and wisdom are in intensive care, hardly breathing. Institutions of higher learning are almost on the throes of death. Places of spiritual retreat are almost waiting for their turn at the funeral bench. Streets are worse than streams of tar; masses who lost their spirit are completely devoid of their feelings of a spiritual

---

9   "Wishing to turn to dust" is in reference to a Qur'anic verse: "...on the Day when every person will see what their own hands have sent ahead for them, when the disbeliever will say, 'If only I were dust!'" (an-Naba 78:40).

quest. Papers, which are supposed to be speaking for the public, are in a wretched condition seeking to play henchman for the devil. In short, it is smoke and dust all around and minds are confused. Spirits and hearts can only be saved by some extra grace. I wish there were a few intellectuals who saw and understood these lines and spoke up! Alas, this absence is another means of grief.

Let us sigh one more time and conclude this article with the following stanza by the Ottoman Sultan Mustafa III, and say farewell to these blessed personages who are closest to God.

This world is coming down, don't think it will be set right in our hands,
Ill fortune passed the authority to lowly ones
Now wandering near the court gates are all jesters
So it seems, nothing but Divine Providence can save us!...

I Pity...

The feeling of pity is the quiver of a person's heartstrings and spirit, a quiver that resonates from a sincere sense of compassion deep in one's soul. Feeling pity, as it were, can be found in all living beings and is a manifestation of many Divine Names of compassion[1]; yet, it is actually a Divine grace special to humanity with distinctive profundities. It is by this extraordinary gift—if a person is not completely distanced from humane qualities—that a person begins to suffer in the spirit and mind before a harrowing scene, immersed in grief and sighs proportional to their sensitivity.

Feelings of compassion and pity are *indispensably* found in all living things, primarily in humankind and especially in parents. All living things try hard to bring an end to whatever causes them to feel pity, even if it means risking and sacrificing one's own life or standing against fires without considering what the consequences could be. When feeling pity, one completely erases from the heart the feeling and thought of living. A hen attacks a cat or dog for the sake of protecting her young; a rabbit ventures death against wolves and hyenas; cattle defy lions or tigers with their horns. And human beings in particular, if they have not lost this magnanimous feeling and inner profundity, will virtually burn from within in the face of scenes that trigger pity; they will dare jumping into fires and walk against death without hesitation when they have this deep sense of pity in their soul.

---

1   Like ar-Rahman, ar-Rahim, al-Hannan, al-Mannan. Each of these names reflect another dimension of God's grace, mercy, and compassion.

Feelings of compassion and pity are directly proportional to how far one has progressed in his or her spirituality. In lofty souls, it goes beyond every frame of reference and reaches to the horizons of those closest to God. They react to selfish considerations like, "fire burns the very spot it falls on," which means that those who really suffer or who can truly understand the misery are only the ones who are directly involved. Instead, they say, "no matter where it falls, that fire burns me up from within!" Thus, they run with humane compassion to extinguish the fire and move people to safety.

In great personages, and more so in prominent ones among them, this feeling is so deep and sincere that they feel agonized on seeing those who suffer. With such an outburst and stupor of compassion, they do not see or feel themselves anymore. Nursi said: "Given that I see the faith of my people saved, I even accede to burning in the flames of Hell. For, as my body smolders in fire, my heart will transform into a rose garden." Such people remind us of the noble Prophet Muhammad, peace be upon him, who returned down to the world after his journey up to the heavens (*Mi'raj*) for the sake of eternal bliss for humanity. These giant figures would throw themselves into the fire to save others. Their feelings of compassion and pity are of a nature to make angels envious and of a quality to serve as an invitation to Divine beneficence.

With a resolution that can only be surpassed by that of a Prophet, they keep running for help day and night, offering prescriptions of all kinds to extinguish the fires of pity. "Here I am," they say with heartfelt compassion, as they knock on every door. "Wake up!" they cry to save those inside, and then they leave only to come back again. They leave as they pass the duty on to the morning breeze to wake people. They do not feel sick of these visits; they are not tired of being spurned with insult and disrespect. Theirs is the road of the Prophets, the road that averts people from Hell and takes them closer to Paradise and beyond; they are aware of the requirements of this path.

The source of inspiration for those distinguished servants was the conscientious magnanimity of Prophet Muhammad, peace be upon him. He had ascended to Paradise to meet with the Divine, reached the Furthest Boundary,[2] and approached the Divine as close as "two-bow lengths" (an-Najm 53:9). The pleasures of our worldly life, even if it lasts thousands of years, cannot even come close to the pleasures of a day in Paradise, nor to a moment in the Furthest Boundary. Having reached these heavenly destinations, the Prophet had the opportunity to stay up there. But he bid a temporary farewell to Paradise and returned to this realm of tribulation for the sake of saving others from falling to the lowest of the low and directing them to the highest horizons. He did it with a feeling of compassion and sense of deep pity special to him, for those who drifted towards Hell. He did it to let others also feel what he felt and allow them to enjoy what he had seen and to present brightness to unfortunate ones in pitiable condition who go through deformations of the heart and spirit.

With such a degree of altruism, while he was giving his loftiest character and mission their due, he was showing the ways to save people from the dark end unbelief is bound for, together with directing them to the ascent leading up to what faith promises. Actually, as that matchless person saw poor souls who had not completely lost their human quality but were struggling in a whirlpool of unbelief and misguidance, he writhed under their situation with a perpetual feeling of compassion and pity; and with that immense spirit of altruism he was blessed with, he would lament for them and immediately call everybody to his radiant course. These sighs had even moved dwellers of the heavens. The following counsel of moderation implied compliment while also reminding him of the frame of his duty and pouring on his blazing heart some water of relief: *"Yet, it may be that you (O Muhammad) will torment yourself to death with grief, following after them, if they do not believe in this Message,"* (al-Kahf 18:6).

Along with similar moderation and counsel, many other elucidating verses of the Qur'an also made reference to his elevated status in this respect and gave a lesson of self-possession to those who took that course. They understood him, received their lesson, and contributed with their voices to that heavenly voice with a consideration of being a vanguard on the way to Paradise. The souls oriented to the lofty circle around the Prophet that followed his footsteps at every issue also showed

2   Sidrat al-Muntaha: The Lote Tree of the Furthest Boundary marks the utmost boundary in the heavens.

the same attitude of beneficence and compassion; they kept sighing by adding new ones to his ballads of pity.

After them, neither did such sighs cease nor the feeling of pity in hearts disappear. New compositions with melodies of the realms beyond were presented to those who staggered on; they were given glad tidings of a blissful future. In the face of those who were taken by currents of unbelief and deviation and were drifting toward the destined fires, everybody was called to help: "Come, fetch water, hurry up! There is fire!" they cried to put off that inevitable end. As the glad tidings voiced compassion, the warnings aimed to stop people's flowing towards Hell. They had belief in God and the Prophet; they saw their thoughts and actions as the necessity of being truly human—which can be in the sense of feeling pity, compassion, or purity of heart—and thus they acted without expecting anything in return. The theme and meaning are from God; the lyrics—as an outcome of their playing the part that falls to their freewill—are from the blessed Prophets and particularly the final one, Muhammad, peace be upon them; and the composition is from those in the blessed "circle" of the Prophet's friends, and from the distinguished servants of God who are overjoyed with beholding the realms beyond the mundane world.

This blessed ember of faith and rushing to help others was so heartfelt and its impact so forceful that it would make the earth and the heavens whirl like dervishes. Those who heard the melody, which sounded as if blown from the Trumpet of Israfil,[3] were invigorated in accordance with the horizons of their comprehension, and, after some continuation, there would come a time when they also contributed to it with the sound of their own hearts. In time, this would turn to a tune of resurrection that resonated in ears. A time would come when those on the road, whose conditions and feelings in terms of human values lagged much behind, also joined this feeling of compassion and pity. This humble author of yours remembers how he once wept for half-an-hour out of compassion and feeling of pity after the death of a bee – it was unthinkable for such a person not to wail on seeing intertwined problems causing different vicious circles of deformation in the world of humanity. By taking these

3   One of four archangels in the Islamic tradition, Israfil's duty is to signal the beginning of the Apocalypse.

into consideration, this humble servant of yours also wished to join that sacred symphony. "I feel pity!" he said as ballads for pitiable ones and offered moans for the waking of those who stumble their way on. He voiced his pity for those who walk in the swamps of unbelief without a purpose and ideal, instead of the blessed course of the Prophets.

The universe as a whole is a grand book of God,

Try any of its letters; the meaning of each reveals nothing but Him.

Recaizade Mahmud Ekrem

I feel pity for those who have been blind all their lives and fail to study this "grand book" of the universe and what lies behind it. I feel pity for those who disregard the Hereafter and eternal life by falling for the outward beauty of this world and its deceptive magnificence and pomp. I feel pity for those who live blind and deaf to eternal life in favor of transient sovereignty and ostentation. I feel pity for the slaves of inferiority complex and who despise their past in slums and now boast of moving from one mansion to another. I feel pity for those out of their mind to the degree of preferring this ephemeral and perishable worldly life over Paradise and Divine Beauty. I feel pity for the thickly heedless, who fell so low as to be bought off for the sake of this short-lived worldly life and fantasies of status, rank, money, and luxury. I feel pity for the dead in their spirit, the unfortunate ones who spend their time laughing and consuming vain entertainment in spite of the present violations of our dignity and honor. I feel pity for the mute devils who do not speak against destructions and irreparable collapses. I feel pity for those who eat, drink, and lie lazily, unaware that they have become no different than beasts. I feel pity for those who appear human physically, yet unaware of the blessing of "the best stature" that the human is and of what being one requires from us. I feel pity for those who first propagated for "rights and justice!" like the Prophets did, but ended up as henchmen of the Pharaoh. I feel pity for those who treat human values like a cheap commodity, at a time when lying is so popular, betrayal is seen as a necessity, and rights are only entrusted to God. I feel pity for the hypocrites who make up religious legitimacy to deceive and slander in their attempt to pass these off as "battle tactics." I feel pity for the so-called religious scholars who let their dignity be trampled under feet with sycophancy for the sake of a cursed reward or a dirty medal. I feel pity for such unfortunate scholars who are bought off with a cheap price to endorse with their approvals (*fatwas*) the killing of innocent believers simply because they are in opposition.

I feel pity for such corrupt scholars who legitimize bribe by classifying it as a gift. I feel pity for those who go astray by turning a blind eye to fraud and say, "let them steal…" I feel pity for the chameleons who – in return for a short-lived worldly rank – do not hesitate to smear innocent people today whom they used to praise to the skies before. I feel pity for those notorious ones oblivious to truth and who declare lies to be true and truths to be lies for fear of losing their benefits and titles, lawful or unlawful. I pity those worshippers of worldliness who turn a blind eye to atrocities not even committed by Crusaders. I pity those hypocrites who use their pen for besmirching people and call this vice a "war strategy."

And I also pity myself for I was overcome by my good opinion of certain people and failed to talk about these atrocities to the masses. I pity myself for mistaking everybody as a friend by disregarding the truth I try to convey in this couplet:

The heart always keeps seeking a true friend

but sometimes one who appears as a friend turns out to be a hypocrite!

I feel deep pain within and sigh for having failed to recognize and having fallen for the faith of a couple of hypocrites. I feel remorse and pain in my bosom for failing to keep up this principle: "Have good opinion of others, yet never give up caution."

I try to find consolation with Bediüzzaman's perspective that "we should view the past and misfortunes from the perspective of Divine decrees." But I still feel pangs of conscience for failing to take a stance in line with the Qur'anic teachings and thus feel to be in a pitiable condition. Although when waves and rays of oppression and malice struck my horizons of thought in a very early phase, I accuse myself for having failed to take shelter in Divine protection in utter confidence in Him and thus I feel agonized with pain.

How I wish that it would have been possible to detect hypocrisy when on the one hand we were being exposed to pompous lip service in regards to human rights, justice, respecting believers, etc., and on the other hand things were shifting towards a disaster like Karbala[4]; then innocent people would not have been martyred and bloodshed would not have amounted to streams. But it is too late; oppression and malice have reached a level to incur Divine wrath. What falls to us after this point is to say, "goodness is in what God has decreed,"[5] by taking shelter in serenity from God (*sakina*), self-possession (*tamkin*), reliance on (*tawakkul*) and submission to (*taslim*) Him, entrusting affairs to Him (*tawfidh*) and utter confidence (*siqa*) in Him, and then expect for extra graces from the Almighty concerning those completely astray; and this should be the very attitude indispensably expected from a believer.

---

4   This is in reference to the heart-rending incident where the Prophet's grandchildren and their company were brutally murdered in Karbala, Central Iraq, in 680 CE.

5   'Ali al-Qari, Al-Asrar Al-Marfu'a Fil-Akhbar Al-Mawdu'a, p. 196; al-Ajluni, Kashf al-Khafa', 1/478-479.

PARANOIA

Paranoia is a psychiatric condition; it is a chronic spiritual illness that disrupts a person's ability for reasoning, balanced thinking, and judgment. Paranoia is a symptom of psychopathy. People who exhibit signs of paranoia, especially those in a leading position, often display the following four common symptoms: 1) They ascribe an extraordinary value to themselves, expect others to do the same towards them, demonstrate attitudes of egoism and egocentrism, and look down on others. Their ego is puffed up even more when others give them what they want. 2) Suspicious of everything, they are constantly distrustful and apprehensive about being wronged. 3) They always see alternative developments around them as conspiracies against themselves, and based on these presumptions they develop aggressive, hostile, and extreme strategies just to be cautious. 4) In fits of delirium, they cause social disharmony, but see themselves as the only one thinking and behaving correctly.

Such people make paranoia one of their ingrained character traits. They are perpetually afraid of losing the things they have somehow obtained. They invent imaginary villains and rebels, and, if they have the power, crush those whom they take as opponents. If they are weak, they side with those who were nothing but a nemesis the day before; they seek to cause perpetual discord and commit the gravest atrocities.

They do not commit hundreds of evils only; as if possessed by evil spirits and devils, they block the good deeds of those who walk on the path of the Prophets. They seek to make those good souls seem like rebels and bandits, while also turning the masses into pawns for their evil purposes. By doing such things they also seek to prevent a global revival of humanity sought by those who strive to represent universal human values in all corners of the world.

On account of what they commit under the urges of the carnal soul and passing fancies, such people disrupt society; ironically, they also cannot obtain their goals, either. To the contrary, with their paranoia-based acts, they have turned their lives and the lives of those around them into Hell.

The main axis of action of a paranoid individual is destruction, which is easily done, but they credit favorable outcomes to their own insight and sagacity. They see others as abnormal—like lunatics do—while they are the ones who continually exhibit all sorts of insanity. By considering those who do not think like them as traitors and terrorists, they live in fear of losing what they possess. Despite special troops they hire to guard them they still don't feel safe.

Paranoids who come from poor backgrounds and obtain important positions and titles later on with a turn of fate are especially seized by every kind of delirium—partially due to their inferiority complex—and a paranoia about losing their power and fortune to others. They are agonized by successions of misgivings. They see angel-spirited people as if they were snakes and set about praising devils.

The Pharaoh at the time of Prophet Moses, peace be upon him, was one such paranoid. Uneasy of the possibility that one day Moses (pbuh) and the Children of Israel could become stronger, he did not only make life miserable for himself and the unwise ones behind him, but also shed the blood of so many people—just like contemporary pharaohs do—committing atrocities of all kinds. When his time was up, destiny removed him from the stage.

History gives us many such examples, and it marks a route of caution for those with insight. Times have their relevant differences of color, pattern, name, and titles, yet within the cycle of historical recurrences, no era was free of such degenerates who looked like humans. From the Pharaoh to Haman,[1] from Nebuchadnezzar to Shapur, from Stalin

---

1   Haman was the high priest in the Pharaoh's court. There are several Qur'anic verses mentioning Haman, like al-Mumin 40:36: "The Pharaoh said: 'O Haman! Build

to Hitler, and to those modern-era Yazid-like tyrants in their footsteps, so many paranoid individuals have come to the fore, performing the same evils and disgracing humanity. They built mansions and palaces for themselves, employed the same wicked ways, and followed the same devilish path. They kept living with misgivings, were haunted by fears of losing the power they had, and to prevent this they defamed and persecuted thousands and millions of decent fellow citizens.

Recent history is full of examples. Hitler left Germany in ruins and killed millions of innocents. In Iran, the Shah – fearing the loss of his power – ruthlessly massacred dissidents. Saddam Hussein, afraid of facing the same fate as the Shah, mowed down those he thought his opponents-to-be. And Qaddafi was no different either; he ravaged his country, all to preserve his own power, in fear of an illusory opponent.

Other paranoids who have emerged like hellish Zaqqum trees in the Islamic world act no differently: people are being thrown in prisons for trivial reasons, mothers and their children are being separated from one another, innocent people are being killed by torture, law and justice are being trampled underfoot. So-called "scholars" serve as Haman, as henchmen to these modern-day pharaohs. Killings and torture go unpunished. Creatures in human form gawk at these; "mute devils" remain silent in the face of injustice and simply watch wicked atrocities without any emotion or action.

Now, the eyes of the oppressed are fixed beyond the horizons as they pray for God's help to free them from their chains. Above all, if only we—as all oppressed and suffering believers—could learn to be content with God's decree and thus not complain about Divine destiny. If only we could internalize the meaning of the prayer *"we are pleased with God as our Lord,"*[2] as also expressed similarly in:

> *Even if it is a hardship from Your Majesty,*
>
> *Or ease from Your Beauty,*

me a lofty tower so that I may attain the ways, the ways of (peering into) the skies, and that I may have a look at the God of Moses, though I surely think that he is a liar."

2   Bukhari, *'Ilm*, 29, *Daawat*, 35, *Fitan*, 15, *I'tisam*, 3; Muslim, *Siyam*, 197, *Fadail*, 136, 137.

> *For our soul, both are serenity*
> *Your Grace is so good, and so is Your wrath.*

Yunus Emre

If only we could feel this sentiment at every breath. If only we could have a deep respect for God and live satisfied with the creed of:

> *Whatever Divine destiny decreed is surely bound to happen,*
> *Commit your affairs to God; neither be grieved nor suffer any pain.*

Enderuni Vasıf

If only we could see that with all these tribulations we are in fact being washed in a pool of spiritual purification, as expressed in:

> *God lets those whom He loves be purified by means of troubles,*
> *Just as pure waters wash away impurities.*

If only we could murmur with this consideration and find consolation. If only we said, "Every oppression and wicked act has a certain term until it incurs Divine retribution," and as a respect to that appointed term, if only we said:

> *A day will come when God will make oppressors say,*
> *"God has indeed preferred you above us."*

Ziya Pasha (with reference to the Qur'anic verse Yusuf 12:91)

Then, we could commit everything to their true Owner. If only we could see the end but not the present, with the belief that, "*Those who rise with oppression are bound to face a terrible end,*" based on the truth, "*unbelief will continue, but oppression will not.*"[3]

If only we could leave everything (beyond our capability) to the All-Knowing One with the belief expressed in:

> *For the oppression of a tyrant,*

---

3   Al-Munawi, *Fayd al-Qadr*, 2/107.

The oppressed has God

Today, it is easy to torment people

Tomorrow, there is the court of God

If only we did not complain while going through temporary misfortunes, and be reassured by the meaning of "God is sufficient for us; what a beautiful guardian is He" (Al 'Imran 3:173). This was the very guideline and constant recitation of great personages; it must be ours as well. Let us say "this too shall pass," and without paying attention to the aspersions by the oppressors and their mouthpieces, we must turn our surroundings into fragrance centers with the rose gardens in our hearts and thus make everyone enraptured and elated.

May God the Kind, Caring, Bounteous and Favoring of infinite Mercy bless us with unshakeable will on this path, a resolute stance, and continuity in our resoluteness.

Inner Decay and Ways to Heal

There is anticipation in the air. People from all walks of life are vigilant, waiting for a ray of light to shine upon them. Their eyes are fixed on the horizon, expecting the rise of a true dawn. Their hopes are spurred at each trace of light in the east. When they cannot see what they were expecting, they sigh with disappointment, yet turn again to their horizon of hope and wonder, "when is the sunrise?" They lower their heads and set sail to another broken dream. Remembering the glorious days of old and seeing the fearful images of today, they sing laments and drift in the high and low tides of hope and despair.

Horrific scenes of disintegration are seen on all sides as we witness more than ever before defiled feelings, darkened spirits floundering in lies, hopes knocked down over and over, dead hearts that do not see and cannot understand, paralyzed souls, trashed consciences that have no horizons and are blind to what lies beyond. Ears are deaf to heavenly voices; eyes – persistently denying their nature – misread and misunderstand laws of creation; minds are intoxicated with positivism, naturalism, materialism, and all that nonsense that do not fit within the framework of reason. Thus buried are the brightest truths in the darkest of the dark and with the darkest of souls. It is like a long gloomy night blackened by pitch-black thoughts of pharaohs.

On the other end of the spectrum, those who can fathom the mysteries and truths of humankind are but a few. Still, as whips lash above their heads, their mouths are zipped up, and their hands are cuffed, all they can do is wait for an extraordinary Divine help. Those who keep their hopes alive move on, saying, "God is enough; the rest is a passing desire." Sometimes, they breathe by uttering the words of the poet:

Let the world come with all its sufferings
Call me a traitor, if I give up my cause for the nation
in the face of any challenge

N. Kemal

Problems have reached the furthest boundaries; brute force is rampant; persecution and violence are blindingly daring; every corner is filled with helpless masses that grieve. The leaders whose hearts have been captured by the devil and the elite who are somewhat lettered but whose eminence is but on the surface do not hear these groans. Even if they hear, they do not care; on the contrary they applaud the tyranny, praise the tyrant, and strive to become like the vizier Haman to the Pharaoh. What is left for the victims, is to suffer and sigh.

God gave humankind reason and heart so we can discover and understand the inner truths of existence. Failing to use these to discern the developments around us and what they stand for will cause us to fail to maintain the quality of *"the perfect pattern of creation"* (at-Tin 95:4); we may not even be aware of this failure. For those who fell from this status, life has been wasted in a vicious cycle of diversions and slips; they confuse the white with the black, the flower with the thorn. For them, the beauty of a rose becomes unfathomable; the songs of nightingale are the caws of a crow. Saving themselves from these crooked thoughts is rare; erring one after another leads them to go lower than their status in creation. While physically they are stuck in pitch-dark thoughts, their spirits drift aimlessly in all directions, and their hearts deform at all levels. They are headed to disintegration and to an inevitable naught.

As a matter of fact, there is a crystal-clear path, a way to be released from these deviations, a path that those who lead a life subservient to their carnality are unable to see. Everything points to the direction of this path in every possible language and discourse. The way out is to know and believe in the All-Glorious One as He is; to look into existence and events with the lens of such a Divine knowledge and make time and again analyses and syntheses accordingly; to explore the natural phenomena with what lies beyond their material being; to study the mysteries that underlie the essence of humankind; to apply mathematical decoding to all the known universe; to evaluate the Earth and all that is found here; and to continue all this intellectual work without a break.

Such firm persistence will lead to a mathematical analysis and exploration of human nature with its physical and metaphysical dimensions. It will turn the human into a projector that will show how to read the book of the universe, for each human is but a comprehensive index of the universe. Reading the book of the universe accurately is a vital prescription for us humans who can reason. This is how we can gather ourselves together, be protected from all kinds of deviations, and will reconquer ourselves. This is how we will be saved from being dragged by whims, will be guided by knowledge, and we will cherish the relief and reassurance of turning to the One. Eventually we will love Him, and will sing songs of love of and reunion with Him.

Unless there is a special Divine grace, it is not possible for the unfortunate ones who are unable to read and discover their profound nature to know and love the uniquely Faithful Beloved, to surpass their physical and carnal aspects and move forward in accordance with the purpose of their creation, to overcome all humanly errors and rise for a reunion with Him.

The path to attaining knowledge of the Unique Truth and to be guided to Him require engaging in serious contemplation and deep thinking, and thereby reaching accurate assessments about one's self. Such a frame of mind becomes a means for the gifts of faith and Divine knowledge, which all together will be of service to the person, allowing them to fathom their reason for existing, what they are expected to do with this life, and the content of the Divine message brought to us by the Prophets. Then they start becoming aware of their status vis-à-vis all of existence, turning their faces gradually in the right direction. Having grasped their purpose, they let themselves flow with the current leading to the Ultimate Purpose. The journey becomes paths of discovery, as the person realizes all material and spiritual depths are the keys to the mystery of existence. They start hearing invitations from deeper realities at each departure from the shore towards the endless horizons, turning their back on all those that are destined to disappear. They build greenhouses against disintegration and hold themselves to account on how to live and behave. As they strain further in their spiritual struggle, they prove themselves as role models and sing the hymns of the dawn to awaken those who are asleep. They guide to God those who can purify themselves from arrogance, vanity, and narcissism.

Conversely, there are those unwise souls who think looking is the same as seeing. They are unable to hear the humming of all that exists in all corners of the universe in their unique languages of disposition; they cannot comprehend their precious status in the midst of everything. They keep their ears closed to sounds and tunes from what lies beyond the physical realms. Theirs is the life of the blind and the deaf. While every letter of the universe cries out for the One, they are far from understanding it. Deprived of senses and enthusiasm, these unfortunate souls live like moving corpses who regret the inner pains of their contradictions.

The discovery of phenomena occurs via discovery of one's self. The human mind, spirit, and all other faculties become lenses to see even deeper, spurring feelings that ask for even more. It is without doubt that such a constant search does not go unrewarded, and then the truth of this heavenly word is revealed: *"Those who know themselves begin looking for Me; those who look for Me will surely find Me."*[1] This search is what being in the *"perfect pattern of creation"* entails.

But the humans unaware of their status vis-à-vis the Divine constantly trip; their lives are no different than those of life forms that eat, drink, and sleep, indifferent to the outer world. They are plagued with the pressing fears of eventual ruin. They try to avoid these fears and run away from themselves by seeking fun, drunkenness, and various forms of hypnosis. Theirs becomes a life wasted, and when the time comes, the candle of life is blown out, leaving them in the hands of the inescapable end they have always feared.

Today, there are so many who are navigated not by their reason but the devil, enslaved by their carnal desires, and who have set sail to waters of rebellion. They act in opposition to what their hearts and spirits call

---

1   This quote is narrated in books concerning Sufism as a *hadith qudsi*—a saying whose meaning is from God and wording inspired to Prophet Muhammad, peace be upon him.

them to; their thoughts are paralyzed, and the qualities that make them human have fallen apart.

Good character has disappeared, indecency is everywhere
How many ugly faces
were covered by that thin veil of morals!
Loyalty, honoring covenants, and trust
are nowhere to be found.
Lies, betrayals are all around, and truth is unknown.
O Lord! No strand of hair shudders of this scene,
How disastrous an upheaval this has been.
Religion and faith are no more;
religion is destroyed, faith is a mirage
Let all the pride go and hearts turn mute
When this moral decay is underway,
Freedom is no more!

M. Akif

It is useless to expect anything from those whose knowledge of themselves is the least. Falsehood is disguised as truth and has set its throne in so many hearts. People expect to hear the true message from those who in fact masquerade as elite and are nothing but "merchants of religion"; they are raw in spirit and "mute devils" who turn their faces away from atrocities and say nothing to prevent them, inviting even more trouble. Conspiracies are staged as truth and masses are manipulated so deceitfully that even the devils are ashamed.

All of these negativities started at a time when societies lost their true identities; call it our fortune, or rather misfortune, that our times have witnessed their flourishing to unprecedented heights. It is not what we wish, but it looks like they will continue to shape our future until we patch up the wear and tear of the last few centuries by way of reading once again the true nature of the physical and spiritual dimensions of the human.

The first step of a revival would be to establish our connection with the Divine as His servants and to become aware of our status as humans among all creation. When the fog clears, and we can finally see the true Ka'ba, we will turn in the same direction and seek opportunities of harmony and unity. As we will offer our unity as a call for help and success from the Divine, we will and should aspire to attain our true human status.

Among the major principles of this revival would be to think systematically, look holistically, question the authenticity of our current knowledge, be freed from the disease of imitation, and trample the filth of arrogance, conceit, and egotism under our feet. Those who put themselves first and are chained to their ego are in fact humiliating themselves.

> *You are unaware of yourself, so it seems*
> *O humankind, you think you are a lowly being*
> *If only you knew*
> *Your essence is precious, even more so than angels*
> *Hidden in you are the worlds, wrapped are the universes.*
>
> M. Akif

Those who become aware of their value leave behind their ego and move on so their remoteness to the One is shortened. As they are welcomed by heavenly beings into unreachable horizons, they abandon all worldly recognition and glory and cherish the discovery of their own nature. Then, not only the deceiving beauties of the world, but even the pleasures of the heavens, become invisible to their eyes. They live calling on the One with the words of Yunus: "I need You and You only."

Those who call on the world and are trapped in the beauties of this false life are fooled by assumptions and aspirations of an eternal life *here* and tend to ignore an eternal life *there*. Their minds and hearts are mortgaged by luxurious mansions and fleets of ships they own. I do not want to defile my language for them and leave them with their fate to be recorded on dark pages of history, for this is not what *the cavalries of light* are expecting; with torches in their hands these cavalries are hunting for light and looking forward to whatever God wills for them.

God renders evil good,

Don't think He does otherwise.

The wise will wait and behold His works;

What God will do, let's wait and see

Surely beautiful it will be.

İbrahim Hakkı

So Others May Live

The real, profound worth of life is revealed when one's life is dedicated to the wellbeing of humanity. It thus gains an otherworldly dimension and attains a quality comparable to that of the dwellers of heaven. Centering life around such an ideal renders one's life many times more fruitful. Those awakened souls experience such a state of rapture that it cannot be contained in a single lifetime. Then they begin to feel this cramped world as if it were but one of the spacious relieving climes of the eternal realms. Such individuals aspire to breathe life into everybody. With every revival they inspire, their hearts overflow with exuberance, as if they too are experiencing a resurrection on the path of being a life for other souls. Saving a single person is akin to saving all of humanity, says the Divine word, and this message constantly rings in the ears of their hearts.

Given that even a single human life in this transient world bears this much importance, it is not an exaggeration to say that an endeavor for a worldwide revival is likely to break the scales of good deeds on the Day of Judgment. With a zest for blowing life into others, a champion of revival is ever-conscious of the fact that humanity has been blessed with the "best pattern of creation" amongst all living creatures. Sensing that the consciences of those who are spiritually paralyzed resemble a grim autumn scene, these champions are so compelled by their mission that ceasing it would qualify as a sinful act. They compose melodies of revival from the tongues of their hearts for those in spiritual death throes; they run to help these lost ones, as if running from one intensive care unit to the next.

This exhausting run is nothing to be overstated in their eyes. They spur their free will on toward the horizons of lofty ideals as being truly human necessitates. They serve as guides on this path of idealism for those who do not know the way, blow energy into those weary of walking, and become compasses for the masses who are without navigation. They inspire to bring back to the source of light those who have their backs to the sun and, thus, keep following only their own shadow. These people become a support and prop for those who are weak and prone to stumble, and provide guardianship for those who are left crawling in misery from the impact of various calamities. They try to soothe sobs echoing on all sides, share the troubles of the wearied ones, forbear various separations with the resolve to keep company with the needy, and come between the growls of oppressors and groans of the oppressed. They keep running like firemen to extinguish one fire after another. As this sense of revival and altruism is preserved deep in their consciences, they strive to fulfill this spiritual endeavor in sincerity and only for Divine approval.

A person with this depth of feeling and thought brings to mind the notion of the *"journey from God"* (*sayr anillah*)[1]; they are in a constant state of metaphysical vigilance. Their entreaties are their pain at how to bring happiness to others instead of themselves. They seek to effect peace in the hearts of others instead of self-indulging in the pleasures of this world. They view life always from a perspective of the sufferings and joys of others and build torches along the path of those who try to make their way through darkness. Reaching success is dependent on making others succeed; they regard indifference to laments as akin to being a "mute devil" and see remaining alive as conditional to blowing life into others; they walk on the path of Divine guides to the tutelage of Prophet Muhammad, the Guide of all guides, peace be upon them.

---

1   *Sayr anillah* is a sacrificial journeying of a seeker who has reached a spiritual level of Divine presence, and after that he or she forsakes, as it were, the spiritual pleasures of that station to return to the community to guide them to Truth despite many difficulties.

These actions by champions of revival yield such surprise fruits when the due time comes; they are like a kernel in the soil that flourishes into many ears. It gives messages of being modest to hundreds of thousands of people and encourages smiles all around as hundreds of new ones have begun walking as one.

INDEX